De GUSTIBUS PRESENTS
THE GREAT COOKS' COOKBOOKS

Southwest Cooking

DE GUSTIBUS PRESENTS THE GREAT COOKS' COOKBOOKS

Southwest Cooking

ARLENE FELTMAN-SAILHAC

PHOTOGRAPHS BY TOM ECKERLE

DESIGN BY MARTIN LUBIN

BLACK DOG & LEVENTHAL

NEW YORK

Published by

Black Dog & Leventhal Publishers, Inc.
151 West 19th Street
New York, NY 10011

Distributed by

Workman Publishing Company
708 Broadway
New York, NY 10003

Manufactured in Hong Kong

ISBN: 1-884822-14-2

h g f e d c b a

DEDICATION

I dedicate this book to my family, which loves to eat:

My parents, Adelaide and Stanley Kessler

My sister, brother-in-law, and niece, Gayle, Stanley, and Amy Miller

My Grandma Berdie, who opened my eyes to food

And to Alain Sailhac and Todd Feltman, the two "men in my life who are my favorite dining partners."

ACKNOWLEDGMENTS

During the fourteen-year existence of De Gustibus at Macy's, many people have given their support and encouragement.

First, my profound thanks to all the wonderful chefs and cooks who have taught at De Gustibus at Macy's. A special thanks to the "chile brigade": Robert Del Grande, Dean Fearing, Bobby Flay, Marilyn Frobuccino, Vincent Guerithault, Stephan Pyles, Jimmy Schmidt, Brendan Walsh, and David Walzog.

Thanks to my priceless assistants who are always there for me in a million ways: Jane Asche, Barbara Bjorn, Pam Carey, Corinne Gherardi, Yonina Jacobs, Nancy Robbins, and Betti Zucker.

Thanks to Barbara Teplitz for all her help and support throughout the years, and to Gertrud Yampierre for holding the office together.

Thanks to Ruth Schwartz for believing in the concept of De Gustibus and helping to orchestrate its initiation at Macy's.

Thanks to everyone at Macy's Herald Square who have supported De Gustibus at Macy's since its inception, with special notice to the Public Relations and Advertising Departments who helped spread the word.

Thanks to J.P. Leventhal and Pamela Horn of Black Dog & Leventhal Publishers for providing the vehicle to put our cooking classes into book form and for being so encouraging.

A special thanks to Jane Asche for her help in the beginning stages of the book.

Thanks to Tom Eckerle for his magical photographs; Ceci Gallini for her impeccable taste and prop design; and Roscoe Betsill, whose food styling really took this project to another level.

Thanks for supplying the exquisite props for the photographs to Zona, N.Y.C. and to Catherine Holt.

Thanks to Marty Lubin for his wonderful design.

Thanks to Mary Goodbody, Sarah Bush, Judith Sutton, and testers Deborah Callan and Elizabeth Wheeler for making the book "user friendly."

Thanks to my agent Judith Weber for her help and advice.

Special thanks to Judith Choate, who shaped all my words into meaningful prose and never ceased to amaze me with her knowledge of food and her patience and calm, and to Steve Pool for getting these words into the computer with smiles and enthusiasm.

Heartfelt thanks to the entire Kobrand Corporation, purveyors of fine wine, especially Cathleen Burke and Kimberly Charles for opening the door for the marriage of fine wine and great food for the last ten years.

Finally, thanks to all the faithful De Gustibus customers who have made all our classes spring to life.

Contents

Foreword

Fourteen years ago, the popularity of cooking classes was growing all over the United States. While interest was high, New Yorkers could not always fit an ongoing series of classes into their busy schedules. Demonstration classes seemed to me to be the answer, and De Gustibus was born. What began as four chefs and an electric frying pan on a stage developed into over 350 chefs and cooking teachers demonstrating their specialties in a professionally equipped kitchen for groups of fervent food-lovers.

When we started De Gustibus in 1980, we had no inkling of the variety of new cuisines that would become an integral part of American cooking. Since then, we have discovered New World Cuisine, Florida Cuisine, Light Cooking, Fusion Cooking, Cajun Cooking, Southwest Cooking — you name it! As American and international cuisines have changed and our tastes have broadened, De Gustibus has stayed on the cutting edge of the culinary experience. We have invited teachers, cooks, and chefs to De Gustibus both because of their level of recognition in the food world and because of their challenging, unique, current, and, above all, noteworthy cooking styles.

The goal of cooking demonstrations at De Gustibus is to make the art of the grand master chefs and cooks accessible for the home kitchen. Each chef leads the way, and holds out a helping hand to the home cook. The results depend as much on the cook's wit, self-confidence, and interest as they do on a great recipe. Thus students, and now readers of this book, can learn to master the recipes of the most sophisticated chefs and cooks.

The reason De Gustibus demonstration classes are so popular is that they allow the novice the opportunity to feel the passion — as well as to see each professional chef's or cook's technique, order, and discipline. By seeing how each chef's personality influences the final product, serious home cooks gain the confidence to trust their own tastes and instincts. New and unfamiliar ingredients, untried techniques, and even a little dazzle, all find a place in the amateur's kitchen.

This book introduces some of the best and most popular menus demonstrated throughout the years. Each dish is designed to serve six people, unless otherwise noted. All the menus were prepared in class, and I have done little to alter them other than to test and streamline recipes for the home kitchen. I have also provided each chef's strategy and Kobrand Distributors' wine suggestions with every menu.

ARLENE FELTMAN-SAILHAC
1995

Introduction

De Gustibus Presents the Great Cooks' Cookbooks: Southwest Cooking features the recipes and techniques from pioneers and trendsetters in this uniquely American cuisine. A blending of many influences including Mexican, Asian, Native American, Texan, and South American, Southwest cooking features ingredients that are bold, spicy, colorful, pungent, and intensely flavorful. It incorporates indigenous ingredients used by ancient civilizations with flavors from around the world. Southwest cuisine melds traditional and experimental styles and techniques, layering and balancing taste sensations with strong and vibrant colors and with contrasting textures to create extraordinary dining.

We recognize that even the most serious home cook does not have a battery of helpers waiting to chop, mince, stir, wash, and clean. Food purveyors do not deliver ingredients and provisions to the back door, and stocks and sauces do not simmer all day on the back burner. This, however, does not mean the serious home cook cannot prepare a meal worthy of four stars if he or she learns what every professional knows: Organize! Prepare! Taste! And, above all, trust yourself and don't be intimidated by tradition.

Before working with Brendan Walsh, our very first Southwest chef at De Gustibus, many of us had not experienced the sensations created by the extensive use of chiles in a refined cuisine. In our first lesson, we learned that it was the flavor of the chiles, not their heat, that created the balance of tastes that so distinctly marks Southwest cooking.

Southwest food has become one of the most popular cuisines featured in our classes, and subsequently, many of the movers and shakers in the "chile brigade" have brought the fire of their passion to our northern urban kitchen. In this book you will find menus from Robert Del Grande, Dean Fearing, Bobby Flay, Marilyn Frobuccino, Vincent Guerithault, Stephan Pyles, Jimmy Schmidt, Brendan Walsh, and David Walzog, so that you, too, can experience the pyrotechnics of these amazing chefs.

STRATEGIES FOR COOKING FROM OUR GREAT CHEFS AND COOKS

Before beginning to prepare any meal, regardless of how simple or how complicated, take the following steps to heart:

1. Read through the entire menu and its recipes in advance.

2. Make as many recipes, or steps, as possible ahead of time, taking care to allow time for defrosting, reheating, bringing to room temperature, or whatever the recipe requires before serving.

For each menu we have provided a feature entitled "What You Can Prepare Ahead of Time." This offers time-saving hints for the cook who is preparing the entire menu, or elements of it, and

Mise-en-place tray

wants to do as much of the preparation before the actual meal. While you may know that many foods taste better fresh, rather than reheated, we have included this list for your convenience to offer *suggestions*, not *required* do-ahead instructions.

3. Place all the ingredients for a particular recipe on, or in, individual trays, plates, or bowls according to the specific steps in the recipe. Each item should be washed, chopped, measured, separated—or whatever is called for—before you begin to cook. This organizational technique, known as the *mise en place* (from the French, it literally means "putting in place") is the most valuable lesson we at De Gustibus have learned from the pros. We strongly urge you to cook this way.

Note that when a recipe calls for a particular ingredient to be cut in a certain size or shape, it matters. The final result is often dependent upon the textures and color, as well as the flavor, of the ingredients. For example, when you make a salsa from this book, you will find the salsa tastes different when the ingredients are all different sizes and shapes compared to when they are a uniform dice.

4. Use only the best ingredients available. All good chefs and cooks stress this. Try to find the exact ingredient called for, but if you cannot, substitute as suggested in the recipe or glossary, or use your common sense.

5. Rely on your taste buds. They will not lie!

6. Don't forget to clean up as you work.

Use the following menu suggestions in full, or plan meals around one or two elements from a menu. Educate yourself, and have fun with new ingredients and flavors. Now you are ready to join the "chile brigade" on a trip through Southwest Cooking.

The Cooks

ROBERT DEL GRANDE
Chef/Owner, *Cafe Annie, Cafe Express*, and *Rio Ranch*, Houston, Texas

STEPHAN PYLES
Former Chef/Owner, *Routh Street Cafe* and *Baby Routh*; Chef/Owner, *Star Canyon*, Dallas, Texas

DEAN FEARING
Executive Chef, *The Mansion on Turtle Creek Restaurant*, Dallas, Texas

JIMMY SCHMIDT
Chef/Owner, *The Rattlesnake Club*, Detroit, Michigan

BOBBY FLAY
Executive Chef/Owner, *Mesa Grill* and *Bolo*, New York, New York

BRENDAN WALSH
Former and original Executive Chef, *Arizona 206*, New York, New York; Former Executive Chef, *Coyote Cafe*, Island Park, New York; Chef/Owner, *North Street Grill*, Great Neck, New York

MARILYN FROBUCCINO
Former Executive Chef, *Arizona 206* and *Cafe Mimosa*, New York, New York

DAVID WALZOG
Executive Chef, *Arizona 206*, New York, New York

VINCENT GUERITHAULT
Chef/Owner, *Vincent Guerithault on Camelback*, Phoenix, Arizona

Techniques

PREPARING CHILES

The intense heat of the chile is mainly found in the seeds, the placenta (the fleshly part near the stem end), and the white veins that run down the inside of the chile. When removing these parts, some cooks prefer to use rubber gloves. Whatever method you choose, be sure to wash your hands well after working with chiles and to keep your hands away from your eyes and mouth until your hands are clean and the chile oil has completely dissipated. Both fresh and dried chiles can be stemmed, seeded, and deveined before use.

THREE METHODS FOR ROASTING CHILES AND BELL PEPPERS

Using a fork with a heatproof handle, hold the chile or pepper close to the flame of a gas burner, without actually placing it in the flame, until the skin puffs and is charred black on all sides. Turn to ensure that the entire chile or pepper is charred. Immediately place the charred chile or pepper in a plastic bag and seal. Allow to steam for about 10 minutes.

Remove the chile or pepper from the bag and pull off the charred skin. Stem and seed. Dice, chop, or puree as required.

If using an electric stove, place the entire chile or pepper in a large, dry cast-iron skillet over medium heat. Cook slowly, turning frequently, until completely charred. Proceed as above.

To roast several chiles or peppers at a time, place on a baking sheet under a preheated broiler as close to the heat as possible without touching the flame. Roast until the skin puffs and is charred black, turning as necessary to char the entire chile or pepper. Then proceed as above.

When roasting chiles, remember that their oils are very potent. As the skin blackens, you may feel burning in your throat and eyes, which may cause some momentary discomfort. When roasting a large number of chiles, it is best to do so under a broiler to contain the potency.

TOASTING CHILES

Dried red chiles are often toasted before using. This is done to heighten their aroma, flavor, and, according to some experts, digestibility.

Remove the stem and, using a sharp knife, slit the chile open lengthwise. Remove the seeds and veins and flatten the chile out. Heat a griddle over medium heat until hot. Add the flattened chile, skin-side up, and toast for 4 seconds. Turn over and toast for 3 seconds more, being careful not to burn the chile. The chile should just darken slightly and begin to release its aroma; if it burns, it will turn bitter.

MAKING CHILE POWDER

Using the method described above in "Toasting Chiles," toast the chiles over very low heat for about 1 minute per side, or until completely moisture-free and crisp. Do not burn!

Tear the toasted chiles into small pieces and process in an electric coffee grinder, spice grinder or mini food processor to a very fine powder. Cover tightly and store in the freezer.

MAKING CHILE PUREE

For fresh chiles: Stem, seed, and remove the membranes. Place in a food processor fitted with the metal blade and process until smooth. You may need to add a drop or two of water to create a puree. Use immediately.

For dried chiles: Toast as directed above. Tear into pieces and place in hot water to cover for 15 to 30 minutes (depending upon the age and size of the chile as well as the toughness of the skin), or until the chile is completely reconstituted. Drain well and place in a blender. Process until smooth. Strain through a fine sieve to remove any bits of tough skin. Cover and refrigerate for up to 3 days or freeze for up to 6 months.

TOASTING SPICES AND SEEDS

Toast the seeds and spices in a heavy cast-iron skillet over medium heat, stirring or shaking the pan frequently. Toast for about 2 to 5 minutes, depending on the ingredient, or until it has turned a shade darker and emits a slightly toasted aroma. Toasting will bring out a more intense and, in some cases, even a different flavor. Store tightly covered in the refrigerator, but for best flavor use shortly after toasting.

GRINDING SPICES AND SEEDS

Freshly ground spices and seeds will ensure a fresh and intense taste in the final recipe. Traditionally, these were ground using a mortar and pestle or a grinding stone. Most chefs now recommend using a small electric coffee grinder or spice grinder that is reserved solely for this purpose. Process each ingredient to the consistency called for in the recipe. Wipe the grinder clean after every use and allow it to air for at least 12 hours before replacing the lid. This will assure no aftertaste or carry-over tastes. It's best to grind only the amount you need, as ground spices lose their flavor quickly.

ROASTING GARLIC

You can roast a whole head of garlic (bulbs) or you can cut the head in half, crosswise, or separate into individual cloves.

1 Preheat the oven to 200 degrees F.

2 Loosely wrap the garlic in aluminum foil. Place on a pie plate or small baking sheet. Bake for 1 hour for a whole

head or 15 minutes for individual cloves, or until the pulp is very soft. Unwrap and allow to cool.

For whole roasted heads: Cut in half crosswise. Working from the closed ends, gently push the soft roasted garlic from the skin. Discard the skin.

For individual roasted cloves: Slit the skin using the point of a sharp knife. Gently push the soft roasted garlic from the skin. Discard the skin.

CUTTING VEGETABLES

Cutting into julienne: Using a very sharp small knife, a mandoline, or an inexpensive vegetable slicer, cut vegetables into thin, uniform sticks (usually about ¼ inch thick and 1- to 2-inches long). This process is easiest when each vegetable is first cut into uniform pieces. For instance, trim a bell pepper into two or three evenly shaped pieces and then cut into julienne.

Cutting into dice: Trim vegetables into uniform rectangular shapes. Then, using a very sharp knife, cut into strips ranging in width from ⅛ to ¼ inch, depending upon the size required. Lay the strips next to each other (you can make a few stacks) and cut into an even dice by cross-cutting into squares ⅛ to ¼ inch across. When dicing bell peppers, it is important to trim off all the membranes and ridges so that you have absolutely smooth flesh.

Pantry Recipes

COOKED BEANS
MAKES ABOUT 2½ CUPS COOKED BEANS
PREPARATION TIME: ABOUT 10 MINUTES
COOKING TIME: 1 TO 2 HOURS
SOAKING TIME: AT LEAST 4 HOURS

Cooking dried beans is simply a matter of reconstituting them by soaking and long, slow cooking. You can double or triple the recipe. Cooked beans keep in the freezer for up to 1 month. Lentils and black-eyed peas do not require soaking before cooking.

1 cup dried black, white, fava, or other dried beans

1 Check the dried beans for pebbles and other debris. Rinse them well in a colander. Put the beans in a large pot and add about 10 cups of water (or 10 times the amount of beans). Cover and let soak at room temperature for at least 4 hours. Change the water 3 times during soaking. If the beans are particularly old, let them soak overnight or for 8 hours.

2 Drain the beans, rinse with cold water and return to the pot. Add fresh, cold water to cover the beans by about 2 inches. Bring to a boil over high heat, skim the foam that rises to the surface, and reduce the heat to a simmer. Cover and cook for 1 to 2 hours until tender. Add more water to

the pot as necessary. The beans are done when they are fork tender. Drain and proceed with the specific recipe.

Note: To prepare the beans by the "quick-soak method," put the beans in a large pot and add enough water to cover by 3 inches. Bring to a boil and boil for 5 minutes. Remove from the heat, cover and soak for no less than 1 hour and no longer than 2 hours. Drain and discard the soaking water. Rinse well. This eliminates the long soaking. Proceed with the cooking instructions above.

FLOUR TORTILLAS

MAKES 10 TO 12 TORTILLAS
PREPARATION TIME: ABOUT 10 MINUTES
COOKING TIME: 30 TO 40 MINUTES
RESTING TIME: ABOUT 30 MINUTES

This simple tortilla recipe from Dean Fearing does not require any unusual ingredients or even a tortilla press.

2 cups sifted all-purpose flour, plus additional for dusting
1 teaspoon baking powder
½ teaspoon salt
½ teaspoon granulated sugar
1 tablespoon solid vegetable shortening
Approximately ½ cup warm water

1 Assemble the *mise en place* trays for this recipe (see page 8).

2 Sift the dry ingredients together into a bowl. Cut in the shortening with a fork or pastry blender until the mixture resembles coarse meal. Add just enough warm water to make a soft dough.

3 Turn the dough out onto a well-floured surface and knead for 3 to 5 minutes. Cover the dough and let it rest for 30 minutes in a warm, draft-free area.

4 Form the dough into 2-inch balls between the palms of your hands. On a lightly floured surface, roll out each ball into a circle about 7 inches in diameter and ¼ inch thick.

5 Heat a cast-iron griddle or skillet over medium-high heat. Place a tortilla on the ungreased griddle and cook for about 2 minutes, or until lightly browned around the edges. Turn over and cook for about 1 minute longer, or until the edges are brown.

6 Wrap tightly in foil to keep warm, and repeat with the remaining tortillas. If cooking in advance, wrap in foil and store at cool room temperature for an hour or so, or in the refrigerator for longer, until needed. Reheat, still wrapped in foil, in a 300 degree F. oven for 10 to 15 minutes, or until heated through.

▶ **If these are for chips, undercook the tortillas slightly.**

CORN TORTILLAS

MAKES 8 TORTILLAS
PREPARATION TIME: ABOUT 10 MINUTES
COOKING TIME: ABOUT 35 MINUTES

¾ cup stone-ground yellow or blue cornmeal or masa harina
1 tablespoon plus 1 teaspoon corn oil
⅛ teaspoon salt
About 2 tablespoons hot water

■ Special Equipment: tortilla press, optional.

1 Preheat the oven to 175 degrees F. or 200 degrees F. if that is the lowest setting. Assemble the *mise en place* trays for this dish (see page 8).

2 In a small bowl, combine the cornmeal, 1 tablespoon of the oil, and the salt until just blended. Add just enough water to form the dough into a ball.

3 Divide the dough into 8 even, small balls. Place each ball between 2 sheets of wax paper and flatten in a tortilla press. Alternatively, using a rolling pin, roll out each ball into a circle ⅙-inch thick.

4 Heat a cast-iron griddle or skillet over medium-high heat. Lightly brush with the remaining 1 teaspoon of the oil. Peel off one sheet of wax paper from a tortilla and place it, dough side down, on the griddle. Cook for 2 minutes. Remove the other sheet of wax paper, turn the tortilla over, and cook for 2 minutes more, or until slightly browned and firm.

5 Wrap in a kitchen towel and keep warm in the oven, and repeat with the remaining tortillas.

▶ **If the dough crumbles or cracks around edges while rolling, add a bit more water and reform.**

▶ **If these are for chips, undercook the tortillas slightly.**

▶ **Tortillas may be made early in the day. Store, covered and refrigerated in the towel or in aluminum foil.**

TORTILLA CHIPS
PREPARATION TIME: ABOUT 5 MINUTES
COOKING TIME: ABOUT 3 MINUTES PER CHIP

Corn or Flour Tortillas (page 12)
Oil for deep frying

■ Special Equipment: deep-fry thermometer.

1 Cut the tortillas into quarters or sixths, depending upon the size you want.

2 Heat the oil in a deep fat fryer or deep skillet to 325 degrees F. Add the tortilla pieces, a few at a time, and fry, stirring continuously, for 3 minutes, or until crisp. Using a slotted spoon, remove the chips from the oil and drain on paper towels.

▶ If you don't have a deep-fry thermometer, you can check for proper oil temperature by dropping a 1/2-inch bread cube into the oil. When small bubbles begin to surround the cube and it starts to turn golden, the oil is the correct temperature. Remove the bread cube with tongs or chopsticks.

TOSTADAS
PREPARATION TIME: ABOUT 5 MINUTES
COOKING TIME: ABOUT 3 MINUTES PER TOSTADA

Corn Tortillas (recipe page 12)
Oil for shallow-frying

Heat 1/4 inch of oil in a large, heavy skillet over high heat to 325 degrees F. Cook the tortillas, one at a time, for about 3 minutes, or until crisp and golden. Do not deep-fry. Tostadas are best eaten as they are fried. If this is not possible, drain well and place on a baking sheet lined with paper towels. Reheat in in a preheated 350 degree F. oven for 2 to 3 minutes, or until hot.

We supply standard stock recipes for chicken, turkey, and beef or veal stock used in the recipes. Homemade stock adds a depth of flavor to a dish not possible with canned broth. However, if time is a factor, use canned chicken broth, buying those brands that are labeled "low-sodium." Do not use diluted bouillon cubes; they are excessively salty.

CHICKEN OR TURKEY STOCK
MAKES ABOUT 4 CUPS
PREPARATION TIME: ABOUT 40 MINUTES
COOKING TIME: ABOUT 2 HOURS AND 30 MINUTES

2 quarts (8 cups) water
2 chicken carcasses or 5 pounds turkey bones, cut in small pieces
3 onions, chopped
1 carrot, chopped
2 ribs celery, chopped
3 sprigs fresh thyme
3 sprigs fresh parsley
1 bay leaf
1 tablespoon white peppercorns

1 In a large saucepan or stockpot, combine the water and chopped carcasses. Bring to a simmer over medium heat and skim the surface of any foam.

2 Add the onions, carrots, celery, thyme, parsley, bay leaf, and peppercorns. Bring to a boil, reduce the heat, and simmer for 1 1/2 to 2 hours, skimming fat and foam from the surface as necessary, until reduced to 4 cups.

3 Pour the stock into a fine sieve and strain, extracting as much liquid as possible. Discard the solids. Cool to tepid (this can be done by plunging the stockpot into a sinkful of ice), cover, and refrigerate for 6 hours or until all fat particles have risen to the top. Spoon off solidified fat and discard. Heat the stock over medium-high heat for about 30 minutes. Adjust the seasonings and use as directed in recipe.

4 To store, cool to tepid, cover and refrigerate for 2 to 3 days or freeze in 1-cup quantities (for ease of use) for up to 3 months.

Beef or Veal Stock

MAKES ABOUT 3 QUARTS
PREPARATION TIME: ABOUT 40 MINUTES
COOKING TIME: ABOUT 7 HOURS

¼ cup plus 2 tablespoons vegetable oil
4 pounds beef or veal marrow bones, cut into 2-inch pieces
3 onions, quartered
1 carrot, chopped
1 rib celery, chopped
1 tomato, quartered
1 bay leaf
1 tablespoon black peppercorns
2 sprigs fresh thyme
3 cloves garlic, crushed
Approximately 16 cups water

1 Preheat the oven to 450 degrees F.

2 Using ¼ cup of oil, lightly oil the bones. Spread the bones in a single layer in a large roasting pan. Roast the bones, turning occasionally, for 20 minutes or until bones are dark golden brown on all sides.

3 Transfer the bones to a large saucepan or stockpot. Add the remaining oil to roasting pan and stir in the onions, carrot, celery, and tomato. Cook on top of the stove for about 15 minutes over medium-high heat until brown, stirring frequently.

4 With a slotted spoon, transfer the vegetables to the stockpot. Add the bay leaf, peppercorns, thyme, and garlic.

5 Pour off the fat from the roasting pan and discard. Return the pan to moderate heat and deglaze it with 2 cups of water, scraping up any particles sticking to the bottom. Remove from the heat and add this liquid to the stockpot. Pour enough of the remaining water into the stockpot to cover the bones by 2 inches. Bring to a boil, reduce the heat, and let the stock barely simmer, uncovered, for 6 hours, skimming fat and foam from the surface as necessary. Remove from the heat. Cool slightly and chill in the refrigerator for 12 hours or overnight.

6 Pour the stock through a fine sieve into a clean pan. Discard the solids. Spoon off any trace of fat. Place stockpot over high heat and bring stock to a rolling boil. Lower heat and simmer for 30 minutes or until flavor is full-bodied and liquid has slightly reduced. Use as directed in the recipe.

7 To store, cool to tepid (this can be done by plunging the stockpot into a sinkful of ice), cover, and refrigerate for 2 to 3 days or freeze in 1-cup quantities (for ease of use) for up to 3 months.

Fish Stock

MAKES ABOUT 3 CUPS
PREPARATION TIME: ABOUT 20 MINUTES
COOKING TIME: ABOUT 25 MINUTES

Making fish stock is easier and faster than making chicken or beef stock. Substituting a canned broth is tricky in recipes calling for fish stock but if you have no time to make stock, substitute low-sodium canned chicken broth for fish stock.

2 sprigs fresh parsley
2 sprigs fresh thyme
1 small bay leaf
2 pounds fish bones (saltwater fish such as sole, John Dory, turbot, halibut, or other very fresh, non-oily fish), cut into pieces
2 tablespoons canola or other flavorless oil
1 small onion, chopped
1 small rib celery, chopped
1 cup dry white wine

1 Make a bouquet garni by tying together with kitchen twine the parsley, thyme, and bay leaf. Set aside.

2 Clean the fish bones under cold running water, removing the gills from the head and any traces of blood.

3 Heat the oil in a large saucepan or stockpot over medium heat. Add the fish bones and vegetables. Lower the heat and lay a piece of wax paper directly on bones and vegetables in the pan. Cook for 10 minutes, stirring once or twice to prevent browning. Be careful not to push the paper into the pan.

4 Remove the wax paper. Add the wine, and enough water to cover the bones and vegetables by 2 inches. Add the bouquet garni. Increase the heat to high and bring to a boil. Skim the surface of all foam. Lower the heat and simmer for 20 to 25 minutes.

5 Strain the stock through an extra-fine sieve. Discard the solids. Use as directed in recipe, or to store, cool to tepid, (this can be done by plunging the stockpot into a sinkful of ice) cover tightly, and refrigerate for 2 to 3 days or freeze in cup quantities (for ease of use) for up to 3 weeks.

ACHIOTE PASTE

MAKES ABOUT ½ CUP
PREPARATION TIME: ABOUT 15 MINUTES
STANDING TIME: AT LEAST SEVERAL HOURS

1 tablespoon achiote seeds
1 teaspoon black peppercorns
1 teaspoon dried oregano
4 whole cloves
½ teaspoon cumin seeds
1 one-inch piece of cinnamon stick
1 teaspoon coriander seeds
1 teaspoon salt
5 cloves garlic, minced
2 tablespoons cider vinegar
1½ teaspoons all-purpose flour

1 Assemble the *mise en place* trays for this recipe (see page 8).

2 Put the achiote, peppercorns, oregano, cloves, cumin, cinnamon, and coriander into an electric coffee grinder, spice grinder, or mini food processor and process until fine. Transfer to a small bowl and stir in the salt.

3 Place the garlic in another small bowl and sprinkle with 2 teaspoons of the ground spices. Using the back of a spoon, mash the garlic and spice mixture into a smooth paste. Blend in the remaining spice mixture, the vinegar, and flour. Scrape into a glass or ceramic container with a lid. Let stand at room temperature for several hours, or overnight, before using. Store tightly covered in the refrigerator for up to 3 months.

CHILE-FLAVORED VINEGAR

MAKES ABOUT 2 CUPS
PREPARATION TIME: ABOUT 5 MINUTES
STANDING TIME: ABOUT 1 WEEK

To make this vinegar, select a dried red chile with the amount of "heat" you prefer. There is no need to remove the seeds from the chiles unless you want to. Likewise, there is no need to remove the chiles from the vinegar after they have soaked in it.

2 cups good-quality white wine vinegar
2 green chiles, halved lengthwise
1 small dried red chile
1 clove garlic

Combine all the ingredients in a glass jar with a tight-fitting lid. Let sit in a cool dark place for 1 week before using. Store in the refrigerator for up to 6 months.

A COLD-WEATHER DINNER
FOR CLOSE FRIENDS

*Cream Biscuits with Barbecued Crabmeat
and Buttermilk Dressing*

Roasted Pork Loin with Acorn Squash Torte and Red Chile Sauce

Banana Cocoa Cake

WINE SUGGESTIONS:

California Reserve Chardonnay (*first course*)

Beaujolais-Villages (*second course*)

Ruby Port (*dessert*)

WHAT YOU CAN PREPARE AHEAD OF TIME

Up to 1 week ahead: Prepare the Barbecue Spice for the crab. Store in a small screw-top jar (a baby food jar is ideal).

Up to 3 days ahead: Prepare the Chicken Stock (if making your own). Prepare the Red Chile Sauce. Cover and refrigerate.

The night before: Bake the Banana Cocoa Cake.

Early in the day: Wash and dry all the herbs, vegetables, and greens. Wrap separately in wet paper towels, place in a sealed plastic bag, and refrigerate. Toast, stem, and seed all the dried chiles. Toast the pumpkin seeds. Pick over the crabmeat. Cover and refrigerate. Bake the acorn squash. Scrape the flesh into a bowl. Cover and reserve.

In the afternoon: Prepare the Acorn Squash Torte up to the addition of the eggs. Cover and refrigerate.

Just before the party: Mix the dough for the Cream Biscuits and refrigerate it. Do not bake until 10 to 15 minutes before serving. Make the Buttermilk Dressing. Cover and chill in the refrigerator for no longer than 1 hour.

Whenever Robert Del Grande visits the De Gustibus classroom, we prepare for an extraordinary experience. Trained as a biochemist, Robert came to cooking through fate rather than design. Because of this orientation, he is constantly experimenting with combinations of flavors and textures, attempting to create simple foods with maximum taste. His uncommon sense of humor only adds to Robert's prodigious classes—we all laugh a lot as we marvel at his novel path to exuberant meals.

Robert inspired a De Gustibus student, Frank Ball, to create a book and videotape called *Trucs of the Trade.* "Truc" is French for a trick or a shortcut. Robert's "truc" for removing a seed from an avocado without inadvertently making guacamole made Frank realize that many professional chefs must have similar "trucs" that could be shared with home cooks. Frank and I gathered 101 tricks from professional cooks from all over the country. With publication of the book, we were able to support the work of Share Our Strength, a network of food industry and other creative professionals united to fight hunger throughout the world. Thanks, Robert!

The commentary preceding some of the recipes comes directly from the chef's mouth. You'll quickly see that Robert has his own special way of introducing dishes.

◁ **Roasted Pork Loin with Acorn Squash Torte and Red Chile Sauce**

ROBERT DEL GRANDE: Cream Biscuits with Barbecued Crabmeat and Buttermilk Dressing

Cream Biscuits with Barbecued Crabmeat and Buttermilk Dressing

"Imagine this: A petite cream biscuit, hot from the oven, its heady aroma of toasted butter and flour startling those quiescent memories of youth. Still hot to the touch, gingerly split equatorially. On the bottom half of such a tender pastry, centered on a huge white plate, is placed some peppery arugula (glistening from a deft treatment with olive oil) and nestled on this, pan-seared crabmeat redolent of barbecued spice and fresh lime. Ah ha…is the picture becoming clearer…le petite biscuit farci?…"

–ROBERT DEL GRANDE

1/2 pound fresh lump crabmeat
2 tablespoons plus 1 1/2 teaspoons Barbecue Spice (recipe follows)
2 tablespoons unsalted butter
1 bunch arugula, washed, trimmed, and dried
1 tablespoon olive oil
Salt and freshly ground black pepper to taste
6 Cream Biscuits, freshly baked (recipe follows)
Buttermilk Dressing (recipe follows)
Tabasco to taste
6 sprigs fresh cilantro
6 lime wedges

1 Assemble the *mise en place* trays for this recipe (see page 8).

2 Pick over the crabmeat to remove any shell and cartilage. Set aside 1 tablespoon of the Barbecue Spice for garnish.

3 In a bowl, combine the crabmeat with the remaining 1 tablespoon plus 1 1/2 teaspoons Barbecue Spice and toss to mix. In a medium-sized skillet melt the butter over medium heat. Add the seasoned crabmeat and sauté for 1 minute, or until just heated through. Remove from the heat.

4 In a bowl, toss the arugula leaves with the olive oil. Season to taste with salt and pepper.

5 Split the freshly baked biscuits in half crosswise. Place the bottom halves in the centers of warm plates. Place a few leaves of arugula on each biscuit. Spoon equal portions of the crabmeat on top of the arugula. Drizzle with a little of the Buttermilk Dressing. Place the biscuit tops over the crabmeat. Lightly dust a little of the reserved Barbecue Spice on each plate. Garnish each biscuit with a drizzle of Tabasco, a sprig of cilantro, and a wedge of lime. Serve immediately.

▶ **Do not dress the arugula more than 5 minutes before serving or it will begin to wilt.**

BARBECUE SPICE
MAKES ABOUT 2 1/2 TEASPOONS

Use the best chile powder you can buy. If possible, buy pure ground chile powder.

1 tablespoon chile powder
2 teaspoons hot paprika
1 teaspoon all-purpose flour
1 teaspoon granulated sugar
1/4 teaspoon ground cinnamon
1/4 teaspoon coarse salt
Pinch of ground cloves
Pinch of freshly ground black pepper

Combine all ingredients in a small screw-top jar and shake to mix. Store tightly covered until ready to use.

▶ **This recipe multiplies easily. Make lots of extra barbecue spice and store, tightly covered, for up to 3 months. Use it to add zest when roasting poultry or meat.**

CREAM BISCUITS
MAKES 10 TO 12 BISCUITS

2 cups all-purpose flour
1 tablespoon baking powder
½ teaspoon baking soda
1 tablespoon granulated sugar
½ teaspoon salt
3 tablespoons unsalted butter, chilled and cut into ½-inch cubes
½ cup buttermilk, or more as needed
½ cup heavy cream
2 tablespoons unsalted butter, melted

1 Preheat the oven to 425 degrees F.

2 In a medium-sized bowl combine the flour, baking powder, baking soda, sugar, and salt. With your fingertips or a pastry blender, blend in the butter until the mixture resembles coarse crumbs.

3 Make a well in the center of the flour mixture and add the buttermilk and cream, mixing just enough to form a soft dough. If the dough seems sticky, add a tablespoon or two more flour. If it is dry and crumbly, add a little more buttermilk. Knead the dough for no more than 2 minutes. Press it out with your hands to a circle about ½ inch thick and 8 inches in diameter. Allow the dough to rest for 5 minutes.

4 Using a 2-inch biscuit-cutter or a glass, cut the dough into circles. Gather the scraps together, press out the dough again and cut out more biscuits. Put the biscuits on an ungreased baking sheet and brush with the melted butter.

5 Bake for 10 to 12 minutes or until puffed and lightly browned. Remove from the oven and place on a wire rack to cool for about 2 minutes. You need 6 biscuits for the crabmeat recipe. Serve the others on the side, or save for breakfast.

BUTTERMILK DRESSING
MAKES ABOUT 1½ CUPS

¼ cup buttermilk
¼ cup heavy cream
2 tablespoons mayonnaise (see Note)
1 teaspoon pure maple syrup
1 teaspoon fresh lime juice
¼ teaspoon salt
Pinch of freshly ground white pepper

1 In a bowl, whisk all the ingredients together until smooth. Transfer to a squirt bottle or a small lidded container. Refrigerate until ready to use, but do not let the dressing sit for longer than 1 hour.

NOTE: For a thicker dressing, increase the mayonnaise by 1 tablespoon.

▶ **Put the Buttermilk Dressing in a squirt bottle, such as those used for ketchup and mustard. Similar squirt bottles can be found in beauty supply stores. This will make it easier to control the drizzle on the crab.**

Roasted Pork Loin with Acorn Squash Torte and Red Chile Sauce

This is a particularly appealing "company's coming" recipe, as there is almost no last-minute work, yet the results are impressive at the table.

2 large acorn squash
1 tablespoon plus 1 teaspoon unsalted butter
2 tablespoons plus 2 teaspoons light brown sugar
1 two-and-one-half- to three-pound boneless, center-cut pork loin, with a layer of fat on top
Salt and freshly ground black pepper to taste
3 poblano chiles, roasted (see page 10), peeled, seeded, and chopped
3 ounces mild goat cheese
¼ cup minced fresh cilantro
1⅓ cups heavy cream
4 large eggs, separated
Red Chile Sauce (recipe follows)
½ cup sour cream
6 fresh cilantro sprigs

1 Preheat the oven to 350 degrees F. Assemble the *mise en place* trays for this recipe (see page 8).

2 Wash and dry the acorn squash. Cut in half lengthwise and scrape out the seeds. Put 1 teaspoon of butter and 2 teaspoons of sugar in each cavity. Set in a baking dish and bake for 1 to 1¼ hours, or until the flesh is soft. Allow to cool.

3 Scrape out the squash flesh into a bowl, discard the skin, and mash lightly with a potato masher or fork. You should have about 3½ cups of squash. Set aside.

4 Lower the oven to 300 degrees F.

5 Season the pork with salt and pepper to taste. Set a large skillet over medium-high heat and when it is hot, sear the pork, beginning with the fat side and then turning so all sides are browned. Transfer the pork to a rack in a roasting pan. Roast for about 1 hour and 15 minutes, until the pork is cooked but still moist and retaining some faint pink color. The internal temperature should be at least 150 degrees F.

6 Meanwhile, to finish making the Acorn Squash Torte, grease a 10-inch square baking dish with butter.

7 Combine the chiles, goat cheese, and minced cilantro with the squash flesh. Season with salt and pepper to taste. Stir in the cream until well incorporated.

8 In a clean bowl, using an electric mixer set on high speed, beat the egg whites to soft peaks. In a separate bowl, beat the egg yolks and then gently fold the yolks into the egg whites. Fold the whipped egg mixture into the squash mixture and pour into the prepared baking dish. Place the baking dish in a larger roasting pan and add water to the larger pan to a depth of about 1 inch.

9 About 25 minutes before the pork is done, remove it from the oven. Lower the oven rack to the bottom rung of the oven and put the pork on it. Position the other oven rack above the pork, leaving ample room for the torte.

10 Bake the torte for 40 to 50 minutes or until set and a cake tester inserted into the center comes out clean. (If you have 2 ovens, there is no need to move the pork to the lower third of the oven. Bake the torte in the second oven.)

11 When the pork is done, remove it from the oven and let it rest for 15 minutes.

12 While the pork is resting, reheat the Red Chile Sauce in the top half of a double boiler over gently boiling water.

13 Spoon equal portions of the torte into the centers of warm dinner plates. Carve the pork into thin slices and fan at least 3 slices around the torte for each serving. Spoon the Red Chile Sauce over the pork. Garnish each serving with a spoonful of sour cream and a sprig of cilantro.

Robert Del Grande: Banana Cocoa Cake

RED CHILE SAUCE
MAKES ABOUT 3 CUPS

6 large Ancho chiles, toasted (see page 10) and coarsely chopped
1 orange, peeled, seeded, and chopped into small pieces
3 cups Chicken Stock (see page 13)
½ cup chopped yellow onion
2 cloves garlic, peeled
Pinch of ground cloves
Pinch of ground cumin
Pinch of of ground cinnamon
2 tablespoons unsalted butter
Coarse salt and freshly ground pepper to taste

1 Put the chiles in a bowl with warm water to cover, and soak for 30 minutes until soft and pliable. Drain.

2 Put the chiles, orange, chicken stock, onion, garlic, and spices in a blender or food processor fitted with the metal blade. Blend or process for 30 seconds, or until smooth.

3 In a medium-sized saucepan, heat the butter over medium heat until it browns slightly. Add the chile puree and bring to a boil, stirring constantly. Lower the heat and simmer for 30 minutes. Taste and adjust the seasoning with salt and pepper. Serve warm.

Banana Cocoa Cake

SERVES 6
PREPARATION TIME: ABOUT 15 MINUTES
COOKING TIME: ABOUT 30 MINUTES

"Here's one for the quick and easy. Sift the dry, mix the liquid, stir it all together and bake. But only if you pass the test that strikes fear in the hearts of doubting cooks: Is a banana dry or liquid, particularly when mashed?…" —ROBERT DEL GRANDE

(Answer according to Del Grande: *liquid*)

1½ cups all-purpose flour
½ cup unsweetened cocoa powder
1 teaspoon baking powder
1 teaspoon baking soda
½ teaspoon salt
1 cup granulated sugar
1½ cups mashed very ripe bananas (about 4 medium bananas)
1 cup milk
8 tablespoons (1 stick) unsalted butter, melted
2 large eggs
1 teaspoon pure vanilla extract
1 cup chopped walnuts or pecans
Confectioners' sugar (optional)
Whipped cream (optional)
Ice cream (optional)

■ Special Equipment: 9-inch square cake pan

1 Preheat the oven to 325 degrees F. Lightly spray a 9-inch square cake pan with non-stick vegetable oil spray. Assemble the *mise en place* trays for this recipe (see page 8).

2 Sift the flour, cocoa, baking powder, baking soda, and salt into a large bowl. Stir in the sugar.

3 In another bowl, combine the bananas, milk, melted butter, eggs, and vanilla, mixing well. Stir into the flour mixture until just combined. Stir in the nuts. Do not overmix.

4 Pour the batter into the prepared pan and smooth the top. Bake for 30 minutes, or until a cake tester inserted into the center comes out clean. Remove from the oven and allow to cool on a wire rack.

5 To serve, warm the cake in a preheated 275 degree F. oven for 10 minutes, if desired.

6 Cut the cake into squares, dust the tops with confectioners' sugar, if desired, and serve with whipped cream or ice cream.

SUNNY AND BOLD, A RED AND YELLOW DINNER

Apple-Cheese Soup

Warm Lobster Taco with Yellow Tomato Salsa and Jícama Salad

Grilled Swordfish with Pineapple–Red Chile Salsa

Brown Butter Berry Tart

WINE SUGGESTIONS:

California Sparkling Wine or Loire Valley Sparkling Wine (*first course*)

California Sauvignon Blanc or Italian Pinot Grigio (*second course*)

California Pinot Blanc or Italian Pinot Grigio (*third course*)

Tawny Port, German Riesling Auslese (*dessert*)

WHAT YOU CAN PREPARE AHEAD OF TIME

Up to 1 week ahead: Make the pastry for the Brown Butter Berry Tart. Wrap tightly and freeze. Thaw just before preparing the tart.

Up to 3 days ahead: Prepare the Chicken Stock (if making your own).

The day before: Prepare the Apple-Cheese Soup through step 2. Cover and refrigerate. Finish as directed in the recipe during the afternoon before the meal. Cut up the vegetables for the Jícama Salad. Wrap separately in wet paper towels, place in a sealed plastic bag, and refrigerate.

Early in the day: Prepare the components of the Lobster Taco. Bake the Brown Butter Berry Tart. Put the Jícama Salad together up to 6 hours ahead but do not season until ready to serve. Cover and refrigerate. Make the Pineapple-Red Chile Salsa at least 2 hours ahead of serving. Make the Yellow Tomato Salsa at least 2 hours ahead of serving.

When Dean Fearing walked into the De Gustibus kitchen for the first time, we thought a Texas rock star had arrived. Wearing red lizard cowboy boots and horn rimmed glasses, and radiating enough energy to light up Macy's windows, Dean was accompanied by his fellow Southwestern chef Robert Del Grande and Mimi, Robert's wife. The three of them were going to prep for Dean's class and then go shopping for guitars! In their spare time, these dynamos had created a small country and western band called The Barbwires, and they were ready to rock. We knew then that this would be a spectacular class—and it was. Dean has since come back often, with incredible results each time.

Dean's menu is a riot of brilliant colors and contrasting flavors, light in feeling and zesty in taste. Many of the recipes can be started the day before, with just some quick, last-minute preparation for completion.

◁ Apple-Cheese Soup

Apple-Cheese Soup

On a cold day, this soup would make a great lunch, especially if served with homemade bread. Dean suggests that if you want a meatless soup, omit the ham and use vegetable broth in place of the chicken stock.

1 bouquet garni (1 tablespoon white peppercorns, 3 sprigs fresh thyme plus 2 bay leaves tied together in cheesecloth)
¼ cup peanut oil
3 ounces ham scraps or 1 ham bone
1 rib celery, diced
2 cloves garlic, minced
2 onions, diced
8 tart apples, such as Granny Smith, peeled, cored, and quartered
1 cup white port
6 cups Chicken Stock (see page 13)
4 slices apple-smoked or hickory-smoked bacon, for garnish
1 small red apple, such as Red Delicious, for garnish
1 small, tart green apple, such as Granny Smith, for garnish
Juice of 1 lemon
4 tablespoons unsalted butter, softened
¼ cup all-purpose flour
1½ pounds sharp Cheddar cheese, grated
Salt to taste
Tabasco to taste

■ Special Equipment: Cheesecloth; fine sieve

1 Assemble the *mise en place* trays for this recipe (see page 8).

2 To make the soup, in a medium-sized saucepan heat the oil over medium-high heat. Add the ham scraps, if using, the celery, garlic, and onions and sauté for about 4 minutes, or until the onions are translucent but not brown. Reduce the heat to medium and add the quartered apples. Cover and cook, stirring frequently, for about 10 minutes, or until the apples soften. Add the port and simmer for 5 minutes more. Add the chicken stock, bouquet garni, and the ham bone, if using, reduce the heat to low and simmer, partially covered, for about 20 minutes, or until the flavors are well blended. Remove the bouquet garni.

3 Meanwhile, in a small skillet, fry the bacon over medi-

um heat for about 5 minutes, or until browned and crisp. Drain on paper towels. Cut into ⅛-inch dice and set aside.

4 Leaving the skin on, cut the green and red apples into ⅛-inch dice to use for garnish. You will need about 2 tablespoons of each color. Put the diced apples in a small glass or ceramic bowl and sprinkle with 1 tablespoon of the lemon juice. Set aside.

5 In a small bowl, knead the softened butter and flour together until smooth to make a *beurre manié*. Whisk the mixture into the soup to thicken it. Cook for 5 minutes longer, stirring frequently.

6 Add the grated cheese to the soup, stirring constantly, until it is melted.

7 Strain the soup through a fine sieve into the top of double boiler set over gently boiling water to keep the soup hot. (Do not press too hard on the solids.) Season with the remaining lemon juice and salt and Tabasco to taste. Ladle the soup into warm serving bowls and garnish with the diced apples and chopped bacon. Serve hot.

▶ If you want to make this soup a day or so in advance, prepare it through Step 2. Cool and refrigerate. Add the *beurre manié,* and then the cheese and seasonings, when you reheat the soup for serving. Do not prepare the apple and bacon garnish until a few hours before serving. This soup can be completed up to 2 hours before serving, but keep it warm in the top half of a double boiler set over hot water. Do not simmer over direct heat after the cheese has been added or the soup will separate.

▶ Cheesecloth is a kitchen necessity. It can be used for making bouquets garnis (cloth-enclosed herb mixtures) so that they can then be easily removed from the pot, for straining liquids, and for lining molds. It is inexpensive and can be discarded after use.

▶ Creamed butter and flour kneaded together is called a *beurre manié* and is used as a quick thickening liaison in sauces or soups. Kneading the ingredients together prevents lumping.

Warm Lobster Taco with Yellow Tomato Salsa and Jícama Salad

SERVES 6
PREPARATION TIME: ABOUT 35 MINUTES
COOKING TIME: ABOUT 25 MINUTES
CHILLING TIME (SALSA ONLY): AT LEAST 2 HOURS

In the off-season, one-pound lobsters may not yield enough meat, so buy one-and-a-quarter-pound lobsters. The recipe calls only for the tail meat and so you will have leftover claw meat. Because the salsa needs to chill, make it before making the taco. The salsa can be made up to 8 hours in advance.

4 one-pound live lobsters
6 seven-inch fresh flour tortillas (see page 12) or store-bought flour tortillas
3 tablespoons corn oil
1 cup grated Monterey Jack cheese with jalapeños
1 cup shredded spinach leaves
Yellow Tomato Salsa (recipe follows)
Jícama Salad (recipe follows)

1 Preheat the oven to 200 degrees F. Assemble the mise en place trays for this recipe (see page 8).

2 Fill a large stockpot with lightly salted water and bring to a boil over high heat. Plunge the lobsters headfirst into the boiling water, cover, and cook for about 8 minutes, or until the shells turn red. Drain and let the lobsters cool slightly.

3 Stack the tortillas and wrap them tightly in aluminum foil. Warm in the oven for 15 minutes, or until heated through. Wrap the hot, foil-wrapped stack in a thick terry towel to keep warm until ready to use.

4 Meanwhile, remove the meat from the lobster tails and try to keep it intact. Reserve the remaining meat (from the claws, etc.) for another use. Cut the lobster tail meat into thin medallions or chop in ¼-inch pieces if it falls apart.

5 In a medium-sized skillet, heat the oil over medium heat. When hot, add the lobster meat and sauté for about 2 minutes, or until just heated through. Remove from the heat.

6 Unwrap the tortillas and lay them out on a work surface. Lift the lobster meat from the pan using a slotted spoon and divide it among the warm tortillas. Sprinkle with grated cheese and shredded spinach. Roll the tortillas into cylinders and place each one on a warm serving plate,

seam side down. Surround the soft tacos with the Yellow Tomato Salsa and spoon a small mound of Jícama Salad on either side.

▶ **If wrapped in wet newspaper, lobsters (and crabs and crayfish) can be kept alive in the refrigerator for up to 4 days. Do not allow the newspaper to dry out.**

▶ **The lobsters can be cooked, cooled, and the tail meat cut up early in the day. Refrigerate until ready to use.**

YELLOW TOMATO SALSA
MAKES ABOUT 2 CUPS

1 pound yellow tomatoes or yellow cherry tomatoes, chopped
1 large shallot, finely minced
1 large clove garlic, finely minced
2 tablespoons finely minced fresh cilantro
1 tablespoon Champagne vinegar or white wine vinegar
2 serrano chiles, seeded and minced
2 teaspoons fresh lime juice
1 tablespoon pure maple syrup (optional)
Salt to taste

In a bowl, combine the tomatoes and their juices, the shallot, garlic, cilantro, vinegar, chiles, lime juice, and maple syrup, if the tomatoes are not sweet enough. Season to taste with salt. Mix well. Cover and refrigerate for at least 2 hours or until very cold.

▶ **For speed, chop the tomatoes in a food processor using on/off pulses to ensure they remain chunky.**

▶ **The salsa can be made early in the day and refrigerated until ready to use.**

DEAN FEARING: Warm Lobster Taco with Yellow Tomato Salsa and Jícama Salad

JÍCAMA SALAD

MAKES ABOUT 2½ CUPS

½ small zucchini, cut into fine julienne about ⅛-inch thick

½ small jícama, peeled and cut into fine julienne about ⅛-inch thick

½ small red bell pepper, seeds and membranes removed, cut into fine julienne about ⅛-inch thick

½ small yellow bell pepper, seeds and membranes removed, cut into fine julienne about ⅛-inch thick

½ small carrot, peeled and cut into fine julienne

¼ cup peanut oil

2 tablespoons fresh lime juice

Salt to taste

Cayenne pepper to taste

In a medium-sized bowl, combine all the vegetables, oil, and lime juice. Season to taste with salt and cayenne pepper. Toss to mix well. Serve immediately.

▶ Although the Jícama Salad may be prepared several hours ahead, covered and refrigerated, do not add the salt until almost ready to serve as it will cause the vegetables to lose their crispness.

▶ A mandoline makes uniform julienne strips from the vegetables.

28

Grilled Swordfish with Pineapple—Red Chile Salsa

This is a wonderfully light fish dish, low in fat and really rich in flavor. It's a spectacular warm-weather recipe and great for summer entertaining. Although not necessary, cooking the swordfish on an outdoor grill allows the flavors of the fish to shine.

6 seven-ounce swordfish steaks, trimmed of skin and dark membrane
3 tablespoons sesame oil
Salt to taste
Pineapple-Red Chile Salsa (recipe follows)

1 Prepare a charcoal or gas grill or preheat the broiler. Assemble the *mise en place* trays for this recipe (see page 8).

2 Brush the swordfish with the sesame oil and season to taste with salt.

3 Put the fish on the preheated grill or under the broiler so that it is 2 to 3 inches from the heat. Cook for 2 minutes, or just long enough to lightly color the side facing the heat. If using a grill, this should be long enough to mark that side with grill marks. Turn the fish over and cook for 2 minutes longer or until the flesh is firm. (To prevent overcooking and keep the fish moist, allow no more than 5 minutes total cooking time for each ½ inch of thickness at the thickest part.)

4 Ladle about ½ cup of the Pineapple-Red Chile Salsa into the centers of 6 warm dinner plates. Place the swordfish steaks on top and serve immediately.

▶ If using an outdoor grill, make sure the grids are very clean. To prevent the fish from sticking, lightly brush the grids with vegetable oil before grilling.

PINEAPPLE-RED CHILE SALSA
MAKES ABOUT 3 CUPS

½ very ripe pineapple, peeled, cored, and coarsely chopped
½ mango or papaya, peeled, seeded, and coarsely chopped
½ red bell pepper, seeds and membranes removed, chopped
½ yellow bell pepper, seeds and membranes removed, chopped
1 small jícama, peeled and chopped
2 teaspoons peeled and grated fresh ginger (from a 3-inch piece)
1 clove garlic, minced
1 serrano chile, seeded and minced
2 dried cayenne chiles, seeded and minced or ⅛ teaspoon ground cayenne pepper
2 teaspoons minced fresh cilantro
2 teaspoons minced fresh basil
2 teaspoons minced fresh mint
1 tablespoon white wine vinegar
1 tablespoon sweet rice vinegar
1 teaspoon soy sauce
1 teaspoon sesame oil
Salt to taste
Juice of 1 lime, or to taste

In a bowl, combine the pineapple, mango, bell peppers, jícama, ginger, garlic, chiles, herbs, vinegars, soy sauce, and sesame oil. Season to taste with salt and the lime juice. Mix well. Cover and refrigerate for at least 2 hours before serving. Bring to room temperature before serving.

▶ The salsa must be made at least 2 hours in advance to allow the flavors to blend. It can be made early in the day and refrigerated until about 1 hour before serving. Allow to come to room temperature before serving so that the flavors are subtle against the swordfish. It does not hold up well for longer than 8 to 12 hours.

▶ For speed, chop the fruit and vegetables—separately—in a food processor using on/off pulses to ensure they remain chunky.

Brown Butter Berry Tart

This luscious dessert is flavored with browned butter scented with vanilla, giving a nutty taste to the berries. After a relatively light dinner, a home-baked fruit tart is always welcome.

TART PASTRY:

1½ cups all-purpose flour
2 tablespoons plus 2 teaspoons granulated sugar
8 tablespoons (1 stick) unsalted butter, chilled and cut into ½-inch pieces
1 large egg yolk
2 to 3 tablespoons heavy cream, chilled

FILLING:

1 pint fresh raspberries, blueberries or blackberries, or a combination of all three
6 tablespoons unsalted butter
1 vanilla bean
3 extra-large eggs
¾ cup granulated sugar
⅓ cup all-purpose flour

■ Special Equipment: 10-inch tart pan with a removable bottom or flan ring

1 Assemble the *mise en place* trays for this recipe (see page 8).

2 To make the pastry, in a medium-sized bowl, combine the flour and sugar. With your fingers or a pastry blender quickly blend in the butter, a few pieces at a time, until the mixture resembles coarse meal.

3 In a small bowl, blend the egg yolk with 2 tablespoons of cream. Make a well in the center of the flour and pour in the egg mixture. Quickly blend with your fingers to form a soft dough. Add more cream if the dough is dry and crumbly. Do not overmix or the pastry will be tough. Roll the pastry into a ball and flatten slightly. Wrap in plastic wrap and refrigerate for at least 1 hour.

4 To assemble the tart, roll out the pastry on a lightly floured surface or between 2 sheets of plastic wrap to 1/8-inch thick and 14 inches in diameter. Line a 10-inch tart

◁ **DEAN FEARING: Grilled Swordfish with Pineapple-Red Chile Salsa**

DEAN FEARING: **Brown Butter Berry Tart**

pan or flan ring with the pastry so that it overhangs the edges by about 1 inch. Trim the edges and crimp lightly.

5 Preheat the oven to 375 degrees F.

6 To make the filling, wash and dry the berries. Sprinkle half of the berries in the bottom of the pastry-lined pan. Refrigerate the remaining berries.

7 In a small saucepan, melt the butter over low heat. Add the vanilla bean and heat gently for about 10 minutes or until the butter turns golden brown, being careful not to burn it. Immediately remove from heat. Let the butter cool until tepid.

8 In a medium-sized bowl, using an electric mixer set on high speed, whisk the eggs and sugar until pale and creamy and the batter forms a ribbon when the beaters are lifted.

9 Remove the vanilla bean from the browned butter. (Rinse, dry and set aside for future use.) Slowly pour the butter into the batter, beating on low speed, until all the butter is incorporated. Gently fold the flour into the batter, taking care not to overmix.

10 Pour the batter over the berries in the tart shell. Bake for 35 to 40 minutes, or until set. Remove the tart from the oven and set on a rack to cool.

11 Arrange remaining berries on top of the tart. Serve at room temperature.

A Cocktail Buffet, Southwestern-Style

*Grilled Tuna Tostada with Black Bean-Mango
Salsa and Avocado Vinaigrette*

*Spicy Chicken, Eggplant, and Grilled Red
Onion Quesadilla with Tomatillo Salsa*

*Roast Leg of Lamb with Red Chile Crust
and Jalapeño Preserves*

Sweet Potato Gratin with Chiles

*Red-Pepper Crusted Tenderloin of Beef with Wild Mushroom-
Ancho Chile Sauce and Black Bean-Goat Cheese Torta*

Blue Corn Biscotti

Maple Sugar-Crusted Apple Pie

Wine Suggestions:

Spanish Cava (sparkling wine)

California Chardonnay

Chilled Valpolicella, Barbera, or Beaujolais

(may be served throughout)

Chef Bobby Flay came to our attention quite by chance. He enrolled in one of our professional classes and then proceeded to query us about the qualifications of the teachers. Bobby was then an unknown chef at the Miracle Grill. Curious about this young man's self-assurance, we went to the Miracle Grill and found that it was, indeed, a miracle. It didn't take long for the rest of New York to discover Bobby's talents. Within three months, he was named the executive chef at the soon-to-be critically acclaimed Mesa Grill, which remains one of the hottest Southwestern restaurants in town.

Since then Bobby has come back to teach many classes at De Gustibus, each one a sellout, each one filled with fans ready to try his tantalizing dishes. We have put together a selection of his recipes to create a really great cocktail buffet for eight people. Bobby has said that no party is worth giving without the host or hostess having to spend a little time in the kitchen to let the guests feel fussed over. We have tried to make this menu as easy as possible, but we think you will still excite your guests with Chef Flay's fabulous creations.

◁ **(From left to right) Spicy Chicken, Eggplant, and Grilled Red Onion Quesadilla with Tomatillo Salsa; Grilled Tuna Tostada with Black Bean-Mango Salsa and Avocado Vinaigrette**

What You Can Prepare Ahead of Time

Up to 1 week ahead: Make the pastry for the Maple Sugar-Crusted Apple Pie. Wrap tightly and freeze. Thaw early on the day of the party. Make the Jalapeño Preserves. Cover tightly and refrigerate. Prepare the Red Chile Crust for the lamb. Cover tightly and freeze. Prepare the Blue Corn Biscotti. Store in an airtight container.

Up to 3 days ahead: Make the Tomatillo Salsa. Store as directed. Prepare the Chicken Stock (if making your own).

Up to 2 days ahead: Prepare the Wild Mushroom-Chile Sauce. Cover tightly and refrigerate.

The night before: Peel and slice the sweet potatoes. Wrap in damp paper towels, put in a sealed plastic bag and refrigerate. Prepare the ingredients for the Black Bean-Mango Salsa. Prepare beans for the Black Bean-Goat Cheese Torta. Cover and refrigerate. Marinate the chicken for the Quesadilla.

Early in the day: Prepare the Black Bean-Mango Salsa. Cover and refrigerate. Bring to room temperature before serving. Prepare the Avocado Vinaigrette. Assemble the Sweet Potato Gratin. Cover and refrigerate until ready to cook. Add 15 minutes to the baking time. Roast the tenderloin of beef. Cool and refrigerate. Bring to room temperature before slicing. Prepare the ingredients for the Black Bean-Goat Cheese Torta. Grill the chicken and vegetables for the Quesadillas.

Up to 3 hours before the party: Assemble the Black Bean-Goat Cheese Torta. Bake the Maple-Sugar Crusted Apple Pie.

Grilled Tuna Tostada with Black Bean-Mango Salsa and Avocado Vinaigrette

This is one of Bobby's signature dishes that offers his exciting execution of contrasts in taste, texture, and color. This vibrant dish makes a terrific appetizer.

2 one- to 1¼-pound tuna steaks, trimmed (about 2¼ pounds)
2 tablespoons vegetable oil
Salt to taste
12 four-inch freshly fried Flour Tostadas (see page 13) or store-bought tostadas
Black Bean-Mango Salsa (recipe follows)
Avocado Vinaigrette (recipe follows)
½ cup diced red bell pepper, for garnish
½ cup snipped fresh chives, for garnish

1 Prepare a charcoal or gas grill or preheat the broiler. Preheat the oven to 350 degrees F. Assemble the *mise en place* trays for this recipe (see page 8).

2 Brush the tuna with the oil and season to taste with salt.

3 Lay the fish on the grill or under the broiler and cook for 1½ to 2 minutes, or just long enough to lightly color the side facing the heat. If using a grill, this should be long enough to mark that side with grill marks. Turn the fish over and cook for 2 minutes more or until the flesh is firm and opaque. (To prevent overcooking and keep the fish moist, allow no more than 5 minutes total cooking time for each ½ inch of thickness at the thickest part.) Cut the tuna into 12 equal slices.

4 Meanwhile, spread the freshly fried tostadas on paper towel-lined baking sheets. Heat them in the oven for 2 to 3 minutes.

5 Arrange the tostadas on a large serving platter. Lightly coat each one with the Black Bean Salsa. Lay a grilled tuna slice in the center. Drizzle the top of each tostada with the Avocado Vinaigrette and then drizzle it in a decorative pattern around the edge of the platter.

6 Sprinkle the bell pepper and chives around the edge of the platter. Serve immediately.

◁ **BOBBY FLAY:** Grilled Tuna Tostada with Black Bean-Mango Salsa and Avocado Vinaigrette

BLACK BEAN-MANGO SALSA
MAKES ABOUT 2¼ CUPS

1 cup cooked black beans (see page 11) or canned black beans, well drained
1 mango, peeled, seeded, and coarsely chopped (about ½ cup)
1 small red onion, diced
½ jalapeño chile, seeded and finely diced
¼ cup lightly packed, chopped fresh cilantro
¼ cup fresh lime juice
2 tablespoons olive oil
Salt and freshly ground white pepper to taste

In a medium-sized glass or ceramic bowl, combine the black beans, mango, onion, chile, cilantro, lime juice, and oil. Season to taste with salt and white pepper.

AVOCADO VINAIGRETTE
MAKES ABOUT 1½ CUPS

½ avocado, seeded
½ jalapeño chile, seeded
2 tablespoons finely chopped red onion
¼ cup fresh lime juice
1 teaspoon granulated sugar
¾ cup olive oil
Salt and freshly ground black pepper to taste

1 Scoop the flesh from the avocado. In a blender or food processor fitted with the metal blade, combine the avocado, jalapeño, onion, lime juice, and sugar. Blend or process until smooth.

2 With the motor running, slowly add the oil and process until the vinaigrette is quite thick. Season to taste with salt and pepper. Transfer to a squirt bottle or glass ceramic bowl. Cover and refrigerate until ready to use.

▶ To facilitate "painting" a design on the platter, transfer the vinaigrette to a squirt bottle such as those used for ketchup and mustard. Similar squirt bottles can be found in beauty supply stores.

Spicy Chicken, Eggplant, and Grilled Red Onion Quesadilla with Tomatillo Salsa

This quesadilla can be served as a zesty appetizer, a main course for brunch or lunch, or a Sunday night supper. Its greatest appeal is that it can be prepared totally in advance and baked at the last minute.

1½ cups Chicken Stock (see page 13)
⅓ cup fresh lime juice
⅓ cup olive oil
3 jalapeño chiles, seeded and sliced
¼ cup chopped fresh cilantro
1 pound boneless, skinless chicken breast (1 whole breast) sliced on the diagonal into strips about 3 inches long and ¼-inch wide
12 ¼-inch-thick slices red onion
12 ¼-inch thick slices peeled eggplant
9 six- or seven-inch Flour Tortillas (see page 12) or store-bought flour tortillas
¾ cup grated Monterey Jack cheese
¾ cup grated white Cheddar cheese
Salt and freshly ground white pepper to taste
4 tablespoons sour cream
Tomatilla Salsa (recipe follows)

1 Assemble the *mise en place* trays for this recipe (see page 8).

2 In a blender or food processor fitted with the metal blade, combine the stock, lime juice, olive oil, chiles, and cilantro. Blend until smooth.

3 Put the sliced chicken in a glass or ceramic dish and pour the chicken stock mixture over it. Cover and refrigerate for 4 hours.

4 Prepare a charcoal or gas grill or preheat the broiler. Lightly oil the grid.

5 Remove the chicken from the marinade and discard the marinade. Grill or broil the chicken for 1½ to 2 minutes per side or until cooked through. Remove from the heat and set aside.

6 Grill or broil the onion slices for 2 to 3 minutes on each side. Remove from the heat and set aside. Then grill or broil the eggplant slices for 1½ to 2 minutes on each side. Remove from the heat and set aside.

7 Preheat the oven to 350 degrees F.

8 Place 6 of the tortillas on an ungreased baking sheet and sprinkle with the cheeses. Top each one with an equal portion of chicken, 2 slices of eggplant, and 2 slices of onion. Season to taste with salt and white pepper. Stack one layered tortillas to make 3 stacks of 2 tortillas each. Top each stack with a plain tortilla.

9 Bake for 8 to 12 minutes or until the tortillas are slightly crisp and the cheeses have melted. Remove from the oven and let rest for about 2 minutes. Cut into quarters, and place a dollop of sour cream on the top of each quarter. Serve hot with the Tomatillo Salsa.

TOMATILLO SALSA
MAKES ABOUT 1⅔ CUPS

8 medium tomatillos, husked, washed, and coarsely chopped
2 tablespoons finely diced red onion
1 tablespoon minced jalapeño chile
¼ cup fresh lime juice
¼ cup chopped fresh cilantro
2 tablespoons olive oil
2 teaspoons honey
Salt and freshly ground black pepper to taste

In a glass or ceramic bowl, combine the tomatillos, onion, chile, lime juice, cilantro, olive oil, and honey. Season to taste with salt and pepper. Cover and refrigerate for at least 1 hour. Allow to come to room temperature before serving.

▷ BOBBY FLAY: Spicy Chicken, Eggplant, and Grilled Red Onion Quesadilla with Tomatillo Salsa

Roast Leg of Lamb with Red Chile Crust and Jalapeño Preserves

SERVES 8
PREPARATION TIME: ABOUT 45 MINUTES
COOKING TIME: ABOUT 1 HOUR AND 10 MINUTES

This is a great dish for a buffet because not only is it good served warm, it is just as tasty at room temperature. Like all the other items on this menu, the lamb makes a wonderful dinner on its own, especially when served with the Sweet Potato Gratin.

1 tablespoon pasilla chile powder (see page 10)
1 tablespoon toasted cumin seeds (see page 10)
2 tablespoons olive oil
Salt and freshly ground black pepper to taste
1 six-pound boned and tied leg of lamb
Jalapeño Preserves (recipe follows)

1 Preheat the oven to 450 degrees F. Assemble the *mise en place* trays for this recipe (see page 8).

2 In a large bowl, combine the chile powder, cumin, olive oil, and salt and pepper to taste. Rub the meat on all sides with the mixture to coat. Let the meat sit for at least 30 minutes and for as long as 2 hours at cool room temperature.

3 Place the lamb on a rack in a roasting pan. Roast for 15 minutes. Reduce the oven temperature to 350 degrees F. and cook for 30 minutes more, or until a meat thermometer inserted into the center registers 145 degrees F. for rare. Transfer the lamb to a cutting board, cover loosely with aluminum foil, and let rest for about 10 minutes.

4 Slice the lamb against the grain into ¼-inch slices and arrange on a serving platter. Garnish with the Jalapeño Preserves.

JALAPEÑO PRESERVES
MAKES ABOUT 5 CUPS

3 red bell peppers, seeds and membranes removed, diced
6 jalapeño chiles, seeded and diced
4 cups granulated sugar
¼ cup red wine vinegar
¾ cup (6 ounces) liquid pectin

1 In a heavy-bottomed, non-reactive saucepan, combine the bell peppers, jalapeños, sugar, and vinegar. Bring to a boil over medium-high heat, stirring frequently to prevent sticking. Reduce the heat to low and simmer for 20 minutes, stirring every 5 minutes. Take care not to let the mixture boil over.

2 Remove from the heat and stir in the pectin. Return the pan to the heat and bring back to a boil. Immediately remove from the heat and pour into a heatproof glass or ceramic bowl. Allow to cool. Cover and refrigerate for 8 hours or overnight before serving.

▶ You can replace the jalapeños with any other hot chile.

▶ For a thicker consistency, increase the number of bell peppers and chiles by 1 or 2 peppers and chiles each.

▶ These preserves make a great hostess gift, packed in a pretty jar, labeled and tied with a ribbon. The preserves keep for up to 1 month in the refrigerator.

◁ BOBBY FLAY: Roast Leg of Lamb with Red Chile Crust and Jalapeño Preserves and Sweet Potato Gratin with Chiles

Sweet Potato Gratin with Chiles

SERVES 8
PREPARATION TIME: ABOUT 15 MINUTES
COOKING TIME: ABOUT 1 HOUR

Zanne Zakroff, executive food editor of *Gourmet* magazine, enjoyed this dish at a class so much that she has since made it part of her Thanksgiving menu. She especially loved the play of the mild sweet potatoes against the smoky flavor imparted by the chipotle chiles. I think it is much more exciting to serve than the traditional holiday potato casserole, and it's always a smash at a cocktail buffet —holiday time or not. If you'd like to go a little lighter, cut one cup of the cream; however, the volume of the sweet potatoes absorbs the richness of the full amount.

3 tablespoons unsalted butter, at room temperature
2 chipotle chiles in adobo sauce (see page 91)
5 cups heavy cream
9 sweet potatoes, peeled and thinly sliced (about 8 cups)
Salt and freshly ground white pepper to taste

1 Preheat the oven to 350 degrees F. Assemble the *mise en place* trays for this recipe (see page 8).

2 Generously butter a shallow 4-quart casserole. Set aside.

3 In a blender or food processor fitted with the metal blade, combine the chiles and cream and blend until smooth.

4 Place a layer of sliced sweet potatoes in the casserole. Pour some chile cream over the top and season with salt and pepper. Continue layering until all the potatoes are used, ending with cream.

5 Bake for 1 hour or until the potatoes are tender and the top is lightly browned and bubbling. Serve hot or at room temperature.

Red Pepper-Crusted Tenderloin of Beef with Wild Mushroom-Ancho Chile Sauce and Black Bean-Goat Cheese Torta

SERVES 8
PREPARATION TIME: ABOUT 40 MINUTES
COOKING TIME: ABOUT 1 HOUR AND 20 MINUTES

This is Bobby's Southwestern version of the classic French steak au poivre. When he demonstrated this recipe in class, he made it in individual portions, but we have substituted a whole tenderloin—easier to serve to a buffet crowd.

6 dried New Mexico red chiles
2 tablespoons cracked black peppercorns
1 seven-pound tenderloin of beef, trimmed
1 tablespoon vegetable oil
Salt and freshly ground black pepper to taste
Wild Mushroom-Ancho Chile Sauce (recipe follows)
Black Bean-Goat Cheese Torta (recipe follows)

1 Preheat the oven to 300 degrees F. Assemble the *mise en place* trays for this recipe (see page 8).

2 Spread the chiles on a rimmed baking sheet and toast in the oven for 1 minute. Remove the stems and seeds, put the cleaned chiles in a blender or food processor fitted with the metal blade and blend or process just until coarsely chopped. The chiles should be approximately the same consistency as the cracked peppercorns. Return the chiles to the baking sheet, add the cracked peppercorns and toss well.

3 Increase the oven temperature to 400 degrees F.

4 Using kitchen twine, tie the tenderloin about every 2

BOBBY FLAY: Red Pepper-Crusted Tenderloin of Beef with Wild Mushroom-Ancho Chile Sauce and Black Bean-Goat Cheese Torta

inches so that it retains its shape while cooking. Rub the tenderloin all over with the oil and season to taste with salt and pepper. Roll the tenderloin in the chile-pepper mixture on the baking sheet.

5 Heat a roasting pan in the oven for 2 minutes, or until very hot. Place the tenderloin in the center of the pan and cook for 12 minutes. Turn the tenderloin over and cook for about 12 minutes more, or until a meat thermometer inserted into the center registers 140 degrees F., for rare. Transfer the tenderloin to a cutting board. Cover loosely with aluminum foil and let rest for 10 minutes.

6 Slice the tenderloin into ⅜-inch-thick slices. Arrange the slices down the center of a serving platter. Top with the Wild Mushroom-Ancho Chile Sauce and garnish the platter with wedges of the Black Bean-Goat Cheese Torta.

▶ **Kitchen twine, or any medium-weight untreated cotton thread, is another kitchen necessity. It is used not only for tying up meat and poultry, but also for bouquets garnis, soufflé collars, and many other tasks.**

WILD MUSHROOM-ANCHO CHILE SAUCE

MAKES ABOUT 4 CUPS

2 tablespoons unsalted butter
½ cup diced red onion
2 tablespoons minced garlic
2 cups red wine
1 cup sliced shiitake mushrooms (about 6 mushrooms)
1 cup sliced cremini mushrooms (about 6 mushrooms)
1 cup sliced portobello mushrooms, cut the same size as shiitake and cremini mushrooms
3½ cups Chicken Stock (see page 13)
¾ cup dried ancho chile puree (see page 10)
2 tablespoons honey, or to taste
Salt and freshly ground black pepper to taste

1 In a medium-sized saucepan, melt the butter over medium heat. Add the onion and garlic, reduce the heat, and sauté for about 5 minutes, or until just soft. Add the red wine, increase the heat to medium, and simmer for about 15 minutes, or until the liquid is reduced to ¼ cup.

2 Add the mushrooms to the pan and cook for about 5 minutes, or until just softened.

3 Add the chicken stock and bring to a boil. Reduce the heat and simmer for 15 minutes.

4 Whisk in the chile puree and simmer for 5 minutes more. Season to taste with the honey and salt and pepper. Serve warm.

BLACK BEAN-GOAT CHEESE TORTA

SERVES 8

1 cup cooked black beans (see page 11) or canned black beans, well drained
1 small onion, chopped
1 clove garlic, minced
¾ cup Chicken Stock (see page 13) or water
1 tablespoon ground cumin
Salt and freshly ground black pepper to taste
20 three-inch fresh flour tortillas (see page 12) or store-bought flour tortillas
2 cups finely crumbled goat cheese
1½ cups finely grated white Cheddar cheese
2 tablespoons olive oil
2 tablespoons ancho chile powder (see page 10)

1 Preheat the oven to 500 degrees F.

2 In a medium-sized saucepan, combine the beans, onion, garlic, and stock. Bring to a simmer over medium heat and cook for about 10 minutes. Drain the beans and reserve the liquid.

3 In a blender or food processor fitted with the metal blade, combine the bean mixture and cumin. Season to taste with salt and pepper. Blend or process until smooth, adding enough of the reserved liquid to make a thick puree. Transfer the puree to a bowl.

4 Spread about 2 teaspoons of bean puree on one side of each of 16 tortillas. Sprinkle equal portions of the cheeses on top. Stack the tortillas so that each stack has 4 tortillas and there are 4 stacks total. Top each stack with a plain tortilla and press down lightly. Brush the tops with olive oil and sprinkle with ancho chile powder.

5 Carefully transfer the tortas to an ungreased baking sheet and bake for 5 minutes, or until heated through, the cheese melts on the inside and the tops are crisp. Cut in half. Serve warm or at room temperature.

▶ **To make 3-inch tortillas from regular store-bought tortillas, cut out a 3-inch circle of waxed paper. Stack 3 or 4 tortillas. Lay the paper pattern on top and cut around it with sharp kitchen scissors.**

Blue Corn Biscotti

Even the pastry chef at the Mesa Grill, Wayne Harley Brachman, gives a Southwestern flair to traditional recipes. Here, the blue corn of the Hopi Indians is used to make fabulous, practically addictive cookies inspired by the famous "twice-baked" Italian biscotti. It's this treatment that gives biscotti their distinctive crispy crunch.

2½ cups all-purpose flour
1¼ cups granulated sugar
½ cup stone-ground blue cornmeal
3 tablespoons stone-ground yellow cornmeal
1½ teaspoons baking powder
½ teaspoon salt
8 tablespoons (1 stick) unsalted butter, at room temperature
2 large eggs
2 tablespoons Anisette or Sambuca liqueur
½ cup coarsely chopped pecans
½ cup coarsely chopped unsalted pistachios

1 Preheat the oven to 375 degrees F. Line a baking sheet with parchment paper. Assemble the *mise en place* trays for this recipe (see page 8).

2 In the bowl of an electric mixer, whisk together the flour, sugar, blue and yellow cornmeal, baking powder, and salt.

3 With the mixer set at its lowest speed, add the butter to the dry ingredients, a little at a time, beating until the mixture resembles coarse meal. Beat in the eggs, one at a time. Stir the liqueur into the dough until incorporated. Stir in the nuts until the dough is thoroughly blended and holds together in a ball.

BOBBY FLAY: **Blue Corn Biscotti**

4 Transfer the dough to the baking sheet and gently press to form a log measuring approximately 3 inches wide, 1½ inches high, and 10 inches long. Bake for about 25 minutes, or until lightly browned. Remove from the oven and allow to rest for at least 2 hours or for as long as 8 hours.

5 Before second baking, reheat the oven to 350 degrees F.

6 Using a serrated knife, carefully cut the log crosswise into ⅓-inch-thick slices. Lay the slices on the same parchment paper-lined baking sheet and bake for 8 to 10 minutes or until lightly browned around the edges but still slightly soft in the middle. For more even baking, turn the biscotti over after 4 minutes. Remove from the oven and cool on the baking sheet.

Maple Sugar-Crusted Apple Pie

There is nothing particularly Southwestern about this pie. It's just delicious and one of Bobby Flay's favorite desserts.

PIE PASTRY:

¾ cup (1½ sticks) plus 3 tablespoons unsalted butter

2 tablespoons plus 2 teaspoons solid vegetable shortening

2 to 3 teaspoons ice water

3 drops fresh lemon juice

2½ cups all-purpose flour

2 tablespoons plus 2 teaspoons maple sugar

½ teaspoon salt

FILLING:

8 or 9 tart apples, such as Granny Smith, peeled, cored, and sliced

¼ cup granulated sugar

2 teaspoons ground cinnamon

1 teaspoon freshly grated nutmeg

¼ cup cornstarch

2 tablespoons arrowroot

¼ cup maple syrup

1 large egg

2 tablespoons cold water

■ Special Equipment: 10-inch tart pan

1 Assemble the *mise en place* trays for this recipe (see page 8).

2 To make the pastry, cut the butter and shortening into pea-sized pieces. Place in the freezer for 30 minutes or until frozen.

3 Combine the ice water and lemon juice. Set aside.

4 In the bowl of an electric mixer, whisk together the flour, maple sugar, and salt. With the mixer at its lowest speed, gradually add the frozen butter. Mix for about 3 minutes, or until the butter begins to break up. Add the frozen shortening and mix for 2 minutes more. Drizzle in just enough of the ice water to cause the dough to come together. Gather the dough into a ball and let it rest for 10 minutes.

5 Divide the dough in half and flatten slightly into discs. Wrap in plastic wrap and refrigerate for 30 minutes.

6 Preheat the oven to 400 degrees F.

7 To make the filling, in a large bowl, combine the apples, granulated sugar, cinnamon, nutmeg, cornstarch, and arrowroot. Genty mix in the maple syrup. Set aside.

8 Roll out half of the pastry on a lightly floured surface or between 2 sheets of plastic wrap to a circle about ⅛ inch thick and 14 inches in diameter. Line a 10-inch tart pan with the pastry so that it overhangs the edges by about 1 inch.

9 Spread the apple mixture in the pastry shell, mounding slightly in the center. Roll out the remaining pastry into a circle large enough to cover the apple filling. Lay it over the filling and roll up the edges of the pastry to make a seal. Crimp them together, trimming off any excess dough.

10 In a small bowl, beat the egg with the cold water. Brush this egg wash over the pastry. Sprinkle with half of the maple sugar. Cut a few steam vents in the top. Bake in the center of the oven for 30 minutes.

11 Reduce the oven temperature to 350 degrees F. Sprinkle the remaining maple sugar on top of the pie and bake for about 20 minutes more, or until the pastry is golden and the filling is bubbling. Serve warm.

▷ BOBBY FLAY: Maple Sugar-Crusted Apple Pie and Blue Corn Biscotti

A MIDWEEK DINNER—
LIGHT, FRESH, AND FAST

*Chipotle-Garbanzo Bean Dip with Blue Corn
Tortilla Chips and Salsa Cruda*

Seafood Seviche with Summer Greens

Achiote-Fried Catfish with Salsa Fresca

Chilled Minted Melon Soup

WINE SUGGESTIONS:

Sparkling Wine (*first course*)

Chilean Sauvignon Blanc (*second course*)

Sancerre or South African Sauvignon Blanc (*third course*)

Late Harvest Muscat or Fruity Chenin Blanc (*dessert*)

Marilyn Frobuccino first taught at De Gustibus after a two-year stint as executive chef at Arizona 206, New York's first Southwestern restaurant. Her approach to Southwestern food was somewhat different from any we had yet experienced at the school. It was as full of flavor, texture, and color as ever, but lighter and easier for the home cook to execute. Marilyn's class left us all feeling that we could go home and cook these dishes one, two, three! This menu really shines when tomatoes and melons are at summer's ripest, but it is an easy one to put together any time of the year.

WHAT YOU CAN PREPARE AHEAD OF TIME

Up to 3 days ahead: Prepare the Chipotle-Garbanzo Bean Dip. Cover and refrigerate. Bring to room temperature before serving.

The day before: Wash and dry the greens for the Seafood Seviche. Wrap separately in wet paper towels, place in a sealed plastic bag, and refrigerate.

Early in the day: The Seviche can be made in the morning, but it must be well drained after 3 hours, or it will continue to "cook" and become mushy. After draining, cover and refrigerate in a glass or ceramic bowl. Prepare the bean dip if not already made. Cover and refrigerate. Bring to room temperature before serving. Make the Chilled Minted Melon Soup. Fry the tortilla chips for the Bean Dip. Store in a dry place or tightly sealed tin. Prepare the Salsa Cruda, omitting the salt. Cover and refrigerate. Bring to room temperature before serving, and season to taste with salt. Prepare the Salsa Fresca. Prepare the seasoning and coating for the Achiote-Fried Catfish.

Up to 2 hours before the party: Season the catfish strips.

◁ **Seafood Seviche with Summer Greens**

Chipotle-Garbanzo Bean Dip with Blue Corn Tortilla Chips and Salsa Cruda

SERVES 6
PREPARATION TIME: ABOUT 25 MINUTES
COOKING TIME: ABOUT 1 HOUR
MARINATING TIME (SALSA ONLY): 1 HOUR

Marilyn's healthful bean dip is perfect for today's entertaining—quick and inexpensive to prepare and low in fat. The chips are just right for dipping and the Salsa Cruda has a vibrant spiciness that people love.

2 heads roasted garlic (see page 11)
2 sixteen-ounce cans garbanzo beans (chick peas), drained, liquid reserved
1 tablespoon canned chipotle chiles in adobo sauce (see page 91), or more to taste
½ cup olive oil
2 tablespoons fresh lime juice
3 tablespoons ground toasted sesame seeds (see page 10)
1 tablespoon ground toasted cumin seeds (see page 10)
2 large radicchio leaves, washed and dried
1 tablespoon salt, or to taste
Salsa Cruda (recipe follows)
Freshly fried Blue Corn Tortilla Chips (see page 13) or store-bought, unsalted chips

1 Preheat the oven to 400 degrees F. Assemble the *mise en place* trays for this recipe (see page 8).

2 Place the roasted garlic, garbanzo beans, chipotle and sauce, olive oil, and ½ cup of the reserved bean liquid in a blender or food processor fitted with the metal blade. Blend or process for 30 seconds or until smooth, adding additional bean liquid (or water) if the mixture seems too thick. Add the lime juice, ground sesame seeds, ground cumin, and salt. Blend or process until combined.

3 Taste and adjust the seasoning with additional chipotle puree, if desired. Scrape into the radicchio leaves and serve with the Salsa Cruda and Blue Corn Tortilla Chips.

▶ The bean dip can be made up to 3 days ahead of time. Cover and refrigerate. Allow it to sit at room temperature for at least 1 hour before serving.

MARILYN FROBUCCINO: Chipotle-Garbanzo Bean Dip with Blue Corn Tortilla Chips and Salsa Cruda

Salsa Cruda

MAKES ABOUT 3 CUPS

8 large, very ripe plum tomatoes, cored, seeded, and cut into ¼-inch dice
4 large tomatillos, washed, husked, and cut into ¼-inch dice
1 pickled serrano chile, minced
¼ cup minced red onion
2 tablespoons minced fresh cilantro
Juice of 1 large fresh lime
Salt to taste

In a medium-sized glass or ceramic bowl, combine the tomatoes, tomatillos, chile, onion, cilantro, and lime juice.

Add salt to taste. Cover and allow to marinate at room temperature for 1 hour before serving.

▶ The smaller and more evenly the ingredients are cut, the more flavorful the salsa.

▶ Pickled serrano chiles are sold in cans in Hispanic markets. If you can't find them, use a pickled jalapeño.

▶ The salsa can be made up to 8 hours ahead of time, covered and refrigerated but do not add the salt until just before serving.

Seafood Seviche with Summer Greens

SERVES 6
PREPARATION TIME: ABOUT 30 MINUTES
CHILLING TIME: ABOUT 3 HOURS

Since the acid in the lime juice "cooks" the fish just as effectively as heat does, seviche is a wonderful addition to the home cook's summer-meal repertoire. Feel free to experiment with other types of fish, or use only one or two of the types listed here if you cannot find them all. A reliable fishmonger will be able to suggest substitutes for the perch or mackerel. Be sure to use the freshest fish available.

½ pound sea scallops, each sliced into 3 equal-sized discs
½ pound ocean perch or red snapper fillet, skinned and sliced into strips about 3 inches long and ¼-inch wide
½ pound mackerel or bluefish fillet, skinned and sliced into strips about 3 inches long and ¼-inch wide
½ pound Atlantic or Norwegian salmon fillet, skinned and sliced into strips about 3 inches long and ¼-inch wide
1 white onion, thinly sliced, halved crosswise
3 cloves garlic, thinly sliced, halved crosswise
1 large red bell pepper, seeds and membranes removed, cut into fine julienne
1 large yellow bell pepper, seeds and membranes removed, cut into fine julienne
2 to 3 pickled jalapeño chiles, seeded and cut into fine julienne
1 tablespoon minced fresh cilantro
1 tablespoon coarse salt
¼ teaspoon red chile flakes
2 cups fresh lime juice (about 16-20 limes)
½ cup extra-virgin olive oil
1 head frisée (curly endive), washed, trimmed, and dried
1 bunch arugula, washed, trimmed, and dried

1 Assemble the *mise en place* trays for this recipe (see page 8).

2 In a large glass or ceramic bowl, combine the scallops, perch, mackerel, and salmon. Add the onion, garlic, bell peppers, and jalapeño and toss gently. Stir in the cilantro, salt, and chile flakes. Add the lime juice and olive oil and toss gently to coat. Cover and refrigerate, stirring occasionally, for about 3 hours until the scallops and fish become opaque.

3 Arrange the frisée and arugula on serving plates or, for a pretty presentation, in parfait or martini glasses. Using tongs or a slotted spoon, place equal portions of the seviche on top of the greens. Serve immediately.

▶ It takes 8 to 10 limes to make 1 cup of juice. You will extract more juice from the limes if you roll them on a countertop, exerting pressure with your palm, before squeezing. Alternatively, place the limes in a microwave oven for 5 seconds on high before juicing. Do not microwave them for any longer—just long enough to warm them a little and release the juice. If you are squeezing the limes by hand, consider wearing rubber gloves, as the 16 to 20 limes you will need produce a lot of juice that can sting small cuts and abrasions.

Achiote-Fried Catfish with Salsa Fresca

SERVES 6
PREPARATION TIME: ABOUT 35 MINUTES
COOKING TIME: ABOUT 40 MINUTES
CHILLING TIME (CATFISH ONLY): AT LEAST 2 HOURS
CHILLING TIME (SALSA ONLY): AT LEAST 30 MINUTES

A southern tradition, catfish is frequently used in Southwestern and Cajun cooking as it readily takes to a variety of strong seasonings. This mild-flavored, low-fat fish is now farm-raised and available across the country.

4 to 5 six- to seven-ounce catfish fillets (about 2 pounds), cut into 18 long strips
2 tablespoons ground annatto seeds
2 tablespoons plus 2 teaspoons chile powder
2 tablespoons plus 1 teaspoon finely minced garlic
½ cup olive oil
4 large eggs
2 cups coarse-ground yellow cornmeal
1½ teaspoons ground cumin
1 tablespoon salt, or to taste
Vegetable oil, for shallow frying
Salsa Fresca (recipe follows)

■ Special Equipment: deep-fry thermometer

1 Assemble the *mise en place* trays for this recipe (see page 8).

2 Rinse the catfish strips under cold running water. Pat dry with paper towels.

3 In a glass or ceramic dish, combine the ground annatto, 2 tablespoons of the chile powder, 2 tablespoons of the garlic, and the olive oil. Add the catfish strips and rub the mixture over the fish. Cover and refrigerate for up to 2 hours.

4 Preheat the oven to 200 degrees F.

5 In a shallow bowl, lightly beat the eggs. In another shallow bowl, combine the cornmeal, cumin, salt, and the remaining 2 teaspoons chile powder and 1 teaspoon garlic.

6 One at a time, dip the seasoned catfish strips into the beaten egg, coating well. Then dip into the cornmeal mixture, making sure all sides are well coated. Place the strips on a wire rack.

7 Heat about ½ inch of vegetable oil in a large skillet over medium-high heat to 375 degrees F. on a deep-fry ther-

◁ MARILYN FROBUCCINO: **Achiote-Fried Catfish with Salsa Fresca**

mometer. Fry the catfish strips, 3 at a time, turning once, for about 6 minutes, or until golden. Drain on paper towels. Put the cooked strips on a wire rack and keep warm in the oven until all strips are cooked.

8 Arrange 3 strips of catfish on each serving plate and spoon the Salsa Fresca on the side. Serve immediately.

SALSA FRESCA
MAKES ABOUT 2 CUPS

1 large, very ripe pineapple, peeled, halved, and cored
¼ cup plus 3 tablespoons extra virgin olive oil
¼ cup fresh lime juice
1 tablespoon jalapeño-flavored vinegar (see page 15)
1 pickled jalapeño chile, seeded and minced
Salt to taste

1 Roughly chop half of the pineapple using a large, sharp knife or a food processor and set aside. Cut the remaining pineapple crosswise into ¼-inch slices. Generously coat the pineapple slices with 3 tablespoons of the oil.

2 Heat a cast-iron skillet over medium-high heat until very hot and smoking. Place the pineapple slices in the skillet and, turning once, sauté for about 2 minutes, or until pineapple darkens. Transfer to paper towels and allow to cool.

3 Meanwhile, put the chopped pineapple in a blender or food processor fitted with the metal blade, and blend or process until thick and smooth. Add the remaining ¼ cup of olive oil and, using 3 to 4 on/off pulses, process until the mixture begins to emulsify. With the machine running, slowly add the lime juice and jalapeño vinegar in a steady stream. Process just to incorporate. Transfer the mixture to a glass or ceramic bowl.

4 Cut the cooked pineapple into ¼-inch pieces. Stir into the pureed pineapple, along with the jalapeños. Season to taste with salt, if necessary. Cover and refrigerate for at least 30 minutes before serving.

Chilled Minted Melon Soup

This dessert soup is immensely refreshing. Made with very ripe melons, it is light, sweet, and the perfect ending to a zesty meal. This soup also serves as a great first course, particularly with the addition of the jalapeño. If you make this in a blender, you will have to do so in batches.

1 five- to six-pound very ripe Crenshaw melon, peeled, seeded, and cubed

1 five- to six-pound very ripe honeydew melon, peeled, seeded, and cubed

3 tablespoons fresh lime juice

2 tablespoons serrano-flavored vinegar (see page 15)

1 tablespoon minced seeded pickled jalapeño (optional)

3 tablespoons chopped fresh cilantro

3 tablespoons chopped fresh mint

¼ teaspoon ground cinnamon

¼ teaspoon freshly grated nutmeg

6 sprigs fresh mint

1 Assemble the *mise en place* trays for this recipe (see page 8).

2 Put the melon cubes in a food processor fitted with the metal blade, or a blender. Add the lime juice, vinegar, jalapeño, if using, the cilantro, chopped mint, cinnamon, and nutmeg. Process or blend for 30 to 45 seconds, or until smooth, adding about 2 tablespoons of cold water if necessary to thin to a soupy consistency.

3 Transfer to a glass or ceramic bowl. Cover and refrigerate for at least 2 hours to allow the flavors to develop.

4 Serve in chilled soup bowls, garnished with the fresh mint sprigs.

◁ MARILYN FROBUCCINO: Chilled Minted Melon Soup

A CELEBRATORY DINNER
FOR NEW YEAR'S EVE

Smoked Salmon Quesadillas

*Sea Scallops with Potato Cakes
and Sherry-Vinegar Dressing*

*Roast Rack of Veal with Parsnip Puree
and Chipotle Beurre Blanc*

Chocolate Walnut Tarte

WINE SUGGESTIONS:

Full-bodied vintage Champagne:
Taittinger Brut Millesiné (*served throughout*)

WHAT YOU CAN PREPARE
AHEAD OF TIME

Up to 1 week ahead: Make the pastry for the Chocolate Walnut Tarte. Wrap tightly and freeze. Thaw at least 1 hour before preparing the tarte.

Early in the day: Make the horse-radish cream for the Smoked Salmon Quesadillas. Cover and refrigerate. Bring to room temperature before using. Wash, trim, and dry all the herbs and greens. Wrap separately, in wet paper towels, place in a sealed plastic bag and refrigerate. Make the vinaigrette for the Potato Cakes. Prepare the Potato Cakes up to cooking. Cover and refrigerate. Prepare the Parsnip Puree. Cool, cover, and refrigerate. Reheat in the top half of double boiler before serving. Bake the tart shell for the Chocolate Walnut Tarte.

In the afternoon: Complete the Walnut Tarte up to 3 hours in advance. Cook the Potato Cakes up to 1 hour before serving. Keep warm in a preheated 350 degree F. oven. (These are best when made right before serving.)

I first met Vincent Guerithault in his adopted home state of Arizona. After working as a chef in cold and wintry Chicago, Vincent yearned for the sunny flavors and warmth of his boyhood in the South of France. During his travels in the United States, he had discovered Arizona. He also "discovered" the unfamiliar ingredients of the foods of the Southwest and immediately got hooked. Teamed with his classical French training, these ingredients offered a whole new way to interpret the traditional recipes he knew so well.

Vincent came to De Gustibus when he arranged a press trip to introduce cynical New Yorkers to his passion: cooking in the classical French manner using the whole range of Southwestern ingredients. We all got hooked on Vincent's new-found style of cooking and on his outgoing personality!

When Vincent joined us at De Gustibus, his fervor excited the classroom. His refined style and use of up-to-the-minute ingredients were all designed to work for the home cook. He made us want to review the classic French recipes—and then be adventurous in adapting them to our favorite flavors.

The menu that Vincent devised for this festive dinner is extravagant yet perfect for a quiet New Year's Eve with good friends, or those times when you want to display how much you care. Much of the prep work for the dinner can be done well in advance, with only a few last-minute cooking requirements for each of the dishes.

◁ Chocolate Walnut Tarte

Smoked Salmon Quesadillas

SERVES 6
PREPARATION TIME: ABOUT 10 MINUTES
COOKING TIME: ABOUT 6 MINUTES

This is Vincent's innovative way of pairing succulent yet conventional smoked salmon with the bread of the Southwest. This recipe can easily be doubled or tripled. Traditionally, quesadillas are folded tortillas. Vincent plays with the concept by serving them unfolded.

2 ounces mild goat cheese
1 tablespoon grated fresh horseradish or well-drained prepared horseradish
1 tablespoon sour cream
1 tablespoon plus 1 teaspoon chopped fresh dill
Salt to taste (optional)
Freshly ground white pepper to taste
3 tablespoons extra-virgin olive oil
3 seven- or eight-inch fresh flour tortillas (see page 12) or store-bought flour tortillas
6 thin slices smoked salmon (about 4 ounces)
1 tablespoon fresh lemon juice

1 Assemble the *mise en place* trays for this recipe (see page 8).

2 In a small bowl, combine the goat cheese, horseradish, sour cream, 1 teaspoon of the chopped dill, salt, if desired, and white pepper to taste. Beat with a wooden spoon until smooth and well blended. Set aside.

3 In a small skillet, heat the oil over medium-high heat for 1 minute. Fry the tortillas, one at a time, turning once, for 2 minutes, or until lightly browned. Drain on paper towels.

4 Spread about 2 generous teaspoons of the horseradish cream on each tortilla. Arrange the smoked salmon over the cheese. Sprinkle with the remaining chopped dill and drizzle with the lemon juice.

5 Cut each tortilla into 6 wedges and serve immediately.

Sea Scallops with Potato Cakes and Sherry-Vinegar Dressing

SERVES 6
PREPARATION TIME: ABOUT 20 MINUTES
COOKING TIME: ABOUT 45 MINUTES

On its own, this appetizer can become a quick mid-week supper for two or three when served with a crisp green salad.

DRESSING:

3 teaspoons sherry vinegar
1½ teaspoons honey
3 tablespoons extra-virgin olive oil

POTATO CAKES:

3 baking potatoes, peeled and cut into ½-inch chunks
1½ tablespoons unsalted butter
2 tablespoons plus 2 teaspoons extra-virgin olive oil
2 tablespoons chopped fresh cilantro
Salt and freshly ground black pepper to taste

SEA SCALLOPS:

6 large sea scallops, about 2 inches in diameter
1 tablespoon olive oil
1 head frisée (curly endive), trimmed, washed, and dried

1 Assemble the *mise en place* trays for this recipe (see page 8).

2 To make the dressing, whisk the vinegar and honey together in a glass or ceramic bowl. Slowly add the olive oil, whisking until thick and emulsified. Set aside.

3 Preheat the oven to 350 degrees F.

4 To make the potato cakes, in a large saucepan, cover the potatoes by several inches with salted, cold water and bring to a boil over high heat. Boil for 20 minutes, or until tender when pierced with a fork. Drain well. Put the potatoes in a medium-sized bowl and add the butter and 2 table-spoons of the olive oil. Mash with a fork or potato masher until smooth. Stir in cilantro, salt and pepper to taste, and mix well. Divide the mixture into 12 equal portions and form each into a patty about 3 inches in diameter.

5 Heat a nonstick griddle over medium-high heat. Brush

◁ VINCENT GUERITHAULT: Smoked Salmon Quesadillas

VINCENT GUERITHAULT: Sea Scallops with Potato Cakes and Sherry-Vinegar Dressing

the griddle with 1 teaspoon of oil. Place 4 to 6 of the potato patties on the griddle and cook, turning once, for 6 minutes, or until golden brown. Transfer to a wire rack set on a baking sheet and keep warm in the oven. Cook the remaining potato patties in the same way, brushing the griddle with a teaspoon of the oil before cooking the next batch. Keep warm.

6 To prepare the scallops, brush them with the olive oil. Heat a nonstick skillet over medium-high heat. Add the scallops and sauté, turning once, for 3 to 5 minutes, or until firm and opaque. Drain on paper towels.

7 Arrange the frisée on serving plates. Arrange 2 potato cakes so that they overlap slightly in the center of each plate. Place a scallop on top, drizzle with the Sherry-Vinegar Dressing and serve immediately.

▶ Keep olive oil in a spray bottle and use it to spray skillets when sautéing. You will use much less oil than when you pour it directly into or even brush it onto the pan.

▶ If holding the potato cakes for longer than 1 hour, reduce the oven temperature to 300 degrees F. to prevent them from drying out.

Roast Rack of Veal with Parsnip Puree and Chipotle Beurre Blanc

Rack of veal is a truly spectacular cut of meat, perfect for special occasions. The beurre blanc adds a bit of smoky taste and a tinge of amber color to the mellow, juicy meat.

RACK OF VEAL:

1 four-pound rack of veal
Salt and freshly ground black pepper to taste
1 tablespoon extra-virgin olive oil

PARSNIP PUREE:

2 pounds parsnips, peeled and cut into 1-inch pieces
1½ cups heavy cream
2 tablespoons unsalted butter, softened
Salt and freshly ground black pepper

CHIPOTLE BEURRE BLANC:

2 chipotle chiles in adobo (see page 91), well drained
1 cup dry white wine
1 cup white wine vinegar
1 tablespoon minced shallots
1 cup (2 sticks) unsalted butter, softened

■ Special Equipment: steamer; meat thermometer or instant-read thermometer; double boiler

1 Preheat the oven to 350 degrees F. Assemble the *mise en place* trays for this recipe (see page 8).

2 Wipe the veal rack with a paper towel and season with salt and pepper to taste.

3 In an ovenproof skillet or roasting pan, heat the oil over medium-high heat until almost smoking. Add the veal and sear the meat on all sides for 4 to 6 minutes, or until well browned.

4 Roast the veal, rib side down, for 1½ hours, or until a meat thermometer or instant-read thermometer registers 150 degrees F. when inserted into the center. Transfer to a cutting board, cover loosely with aluminum foil and allow to rest for 15 minutes before slicing.

5 Meanwhile, to make the parsnip puree, steam the parsnips in a covered steamer basket set over boiling water for 20 minutes, or until tender when pierced with a fork. Transfer the parsnips to a blender or food processor fitted with the metal blade.

6 In a small saucepan, heat the cream over medium heat until small bubbles begin to appear around the edges. Do not boil. Add to the parsnips. Add the butter and salt and pepper to taste, and blend or process for 15 to 20 seconds until smooth. Transfer the puree to the top half of a double boiler over simmering water. Cover and keep warm.

7 To make the beurre blanc, put the chipotles in a blender or food processor fitted with the metal blade and blend or process until smooth.

8 In a small, heavy, nonreactive saucepan, bring the wine, wine vinegar, and shallots to a boil over medium heat. Reduce the heat to low and simmer, uncovered, for 20 to 30 minutes, or until the liquid has evaporated. Whisking vigorously, add the butter, 2 tablespoons at time, making each addition just before the previous one has been totally incorporated. When all the butter has been incorporated, whisk in the chipotle puree. Remove from the heat, cover and keep warm.

9 Slice the veal into chops. Place a mound of parsnip puree in the center of each warm dinner plate. Arrange one or two chops on top. Spoon the Chipotle Beurre Blanc over the meat. Serve immediately.

▶ Because it usually has to be special-ordered from the butcher, replace the rack of veal with a more economical rolled veal roast weighing about 3½ pounds, if you prefer.

▶ If you have difficulty pureeing the small amount of chipotle chiles in the blender or food processor, chop them very fine with a sharp knife.

Chocolate Walnut Tarte

SERVES 6
PREPARATION TIME: ABOUT 30 MINUTES
BAKING TIME: ABOUT 25 MINUTES
CHILLING TIME (PASTRY ONLY): ABOUT 2 HOURS AND 30 MINUTES

When Vincent Guerithault made this dessert in class, we could hardly keep the audience in its seats. Chef Vincent suggests serving this tart with a scoop each of banana and chocolate ice cream drizzled with chocolate sauce. Talk about a sweet death!

TART PASTRY:

1 cup all-purpose flour
1 teaspoon granulated sugar
8 tablespoons (1 stick) unsalted butter, chilled and cut into pieces
2 to 3 tablespoons ice water

FILLING:

1½ cups semisweet chocolate chips
1½ ounces semisweet chocolate, chopped
1 cup walnut halves
1 tablespoon plus 1 teaspoon dark rum
2 teaspoons pure vanilla extract
2 tablespoons unsalted butter
½ cup dark brown sugar
1 large egg, lightly beaten
4 firm bananas

■ Special Equipment: 10-inch tart pan with removable bottom; pie weights or dried beans, peas, or rice

1 Assemble the *mise en place* trays for this recipe (see page 8).

2 To make the pastry, in a medium-sized bowl, combine the flour and sugar. With your fingertips or a pastry blender, quickly blend in the butter, a few pieces at time, until the mixture resembles coarse meal. Add the water, a tablespoon at time, and quickly blend with your hands to form a soft dough. Do not overmix, or the pastry will be tough. You may need additional water, but take care not to allow the dough to get sticky. Roll the pastry into a ball and flatten slightly. Wrap in plastic wrap and refrigerate for at least 2 hours.

3 To make the tart, roll out the pastry on a lightly floured surface or between 2 sheets of plastic wrap to a circle about 14 inches in diameter and ⅛ inch thick. Line a 10-inch tart pan with the pastry so that it overhangs the edges by about 1 inch. Trim the edges and crimp lightly. Prick the bottom of the pastry with a fork. Refrigerate for at least 30 minutes.

4 Preheat the oven to 450 degrees F.

5 Line the pastry with lightly buttered parchment paper or aluminum foil, buttered side down. Fill with pie weights, dried beans, or rice. Bake about 15 minutes or until the edges of the pastry are golden and the bottom is set. Remove the weights and parchment and return the tart shell to the oven for 3 to 4 minutes until lightly browned. Cool completely on a wire rack before filling. (Leave the oven on.)

6 To make the filling, in a medium-sized bowl, combine the chocolate chips, chopped chocolate, walnuts, rum, and vanilla extract. Set aside.

7 In a small saucepan, melt the butter and sugar over medium heat, stirring frequently. Bring the mixture just to a boil. Remove from the heat and pour over chocolate mixture, stirring continuously until smooth and cooled slightly.

8 Mix in the egg, stirring until incorporated.

9 Peel and slice the bananas and arrange them evenly in the baked tart shell. Spoon the chocolate mixture over the bananas, forming a slight mound in the center. Bake for about 4 minutes, or until the top is slightly crumbly. Do not overbake. Allow to cool completely on a wire rack before serving.

▶ **Be sure to let the chocolate mixture cool slightly before stirring in the egg to prevent the egg from "cooking."**

◁ VINCENT GUERITHAULT: **Roast Rack of Veal with Parsnip Puree and Chipotle Beurre Blanc**

An End-of-Summer Southwestern Dinner

*Red Snapper with Mexican Oregano Pesto Sauce
and Jícama-Melon Relish*

*Chipotle Lamb Chops with Creamed Corn Pudding
and Three Tomato Salsas*

*Cranberry-Mango Cobbler
with Cinnamon-Pecan Cream*

Wine Suggestions:

Sauvignon Blanc (*first course*)

Merlot (*second course*)

Muscat de Beaumes-de-Venise (*dessert*)

While organizing cooking classes in Dallas, Texas, a number of years ago, I had the good fortune to eat at two of the most acclaimed restaurants in the city at that time: Routh Street Cafe and Baby Routh. I was immediately struck by the creativity of Stephan Pyles, the chef at both. He brought together a startling combination of ingredients and mixed them with techniques of cooking and presentation that had helped turn Dallas into a food mecca. We enticed Stephan east for teaching demonstration classes at De Gustibus. We quickly found that he was not only a great chef but also a passionate and dedicated teacher more than willing to share his culinary expertise with his students.

The menu he presents here is, in many ways, as elaborate and complicated as the most exalted French meal, but with a very definite Southwestern flair. Color and flavor are dependent on the lushness and succulence of the end-of-summer tomatoes, corn, peppers, and melons. The lamb chops are only heightened by outdoor grilling. What a great way to celebrate Labor Day—or any late-summer weekend!

As delicious as the meal is when served in its entirety, each course can stand on its own so that you can create your own menu if you have less time than this one demands.

◁ **Chipotle Lamb Chops with Creamed Corn Pudding and Three Tomato Salsas**

What You Can Prepare Ahead of Time

Up to 1 week ahead: Make the Mexican Oregano Pesto. Store in tightly sealed jar and refrigerate. Make the Fish Stock (if making your own).

The day before: Scrape the corn kernels from the cobs for the Creamed Corn Pudding. Store in covered container and refrigerate.

Early in the day: Prepare the Jícama-Melon Relish. Prepare the three different salsas. Cover and refrigerate. Bring to room temperature before serving. Bake the Cranberry-Mango Cobbler. Reheat in a preheated 300 degree F. oven for 15 minutes before serving. Store loosely covered in a cool place. Prepare the Cinnamon-Pecan Cream. Cover and refrigerate.

Up to 2 hours before the party: Make the chile sauce for the lamb chops up to the point of adding the butter.

1 hour before the party: Make the butter sauce for the snapper. Keep warm in a double boiler over gently simmering water.

Just before the party: Reheat the chile sauce for the lamb chops. Incorporate the butter as instructed in the recipe. Keep warm over gently simmering water. Measure and assemble the ingredients for the Creamed Corn Pudding.

Red Snapper with Mexican Oregano Pesto Sauce and Jícama-Melon Relish

SERVES 6
PREPARATION TIME: ABOUT 45 MINUTES
COOKING TIME: ABOUT 30 MINUTES

Mexican oregano (found in Hispanic markets), with a somewhat sharper flavor than the traditional Mediterranean oregano, perfectly complements the mild fish.

SAUCE:

⅔ cup Fish Stock (see page 14)
⅓ cup dry white wine
2 tablespoons white wine vinegar
1 tablespoon minced shallots
1 sprig fresh parsley
½ cup heavy cream
1 cup (2 sticks) unsalted butter, softened
1 tablespoon Mexican Oregano Pesto (recipe follows)
1 teaspoon fresh lime juice
Salt and freshly ground white pepper to taste

SNAPPER:

6 seven-to-eight-ounce red snapper fillets, rinsed and patted dry
Salt and freshly ground black pepper to taste
1 cup all-purpose flour
Vegetable oil for shallow frying
Jícama-Melon Relish (recipe follows)

1 Assemble the *mise en place* trays for this recipe (see page 8).

2 To make the sauce, in a medium-sized saucepan, combine the stock, wine, vinegar, shallots, and parsley. Bring to a boil over medium heat and cook for about 10 minutes or until the liquid is reduced to 2 tablespoons. Add the cream and boil for 4 to 5 minutes longer, until reduced by one third.

3 Remove the pan from the heat and whisk in 2 tablespoons of the butter. Return the pan to very low heat and whisk in the remaining butter, a tablespoon at a time. Do not add the next tablespoon of butter until the one before it is incorporated. If drops of melted butter appear on the surface, remove the pan from the heat and whisk to reincorporate the butter. Then return to the heat and continue adding the butter.

4 Strain the sauce through a fine sieve into the top half of a double boiler. Whisk in the pesto and lime juice. Season to taste with salt and white pepper. Set over gently simmering water and keep warm until ready to serve. (You should have about 1½ cups of sauce.)

5 To prepare the fish, season the fillets with salt and pepper to taste. Place the flour in a shallow bowl and lay the fillets in it, one at a time, turning to coat on both sides. Shake off the excess flour.

6 Heat about ½ inch of vegetable oil in a large skillet over medium heat. When the oil is hot, add the fish fillets and cook, turning once, for about 5 minutes, or until golden. Do not crowd the pan; fry the fish in batches if necessary.

7 Drain the fish fillets on paper towels. Place on plates, spoon a little of the sauce around the fish and garnish with Jícama-Melon Relish. Serve immediately.

MEXICAN OREGANO PESTO
MAKES ABOUT 1 CUP

1 cup tightly packed fresh Mexican oregano leaves
2 teaspoons toasted pine nuts (see page 10)
1 clove garlic
¼ cup olive oil

In a blender or food processor fitted with the metal blade, combine the oregano, nuts, and garlic. Blend or process, using quick on/off pulses, until minced. With the motor running, slowly add the oil, processing until smooth. Transfer the pesto to a glass or ceramic bowl. Cover and refrigerate. Bring to room temperature before using.

▶ **Store leftover pesto in the refrigerator in a tightly sealed glass jar or bowl for up to 2 weeks. Use it to flavor mayonnaise-based salad dressings, vinaigrettes, and pasta dishes.**

▶ **If you can't find Mexican oregano use any fresh oregano available**

▷ STEPHAN PYLES: Red Snapper with Mexican Oregano Pesto Sauce and Jícama-Melon Relish

Jicama-Melon Relish
MAKES ABOUT 2 CUPS

Cut the vegetables and melon into the size dice specified. With the exception of the cucumber, which is cut into ⅛-inch dice, the dice should be ¼-inch. For these amounts, buy one whole vegetable, piece of fruit, or melon. You will have leftovers, but buying the produce whole rather than pre-cut insures freshness.

¼ cup jícama, peeled, seeded, and cut into ¼-inch dice
¼ cup cantaloupe melon, peeled, seeded, and cut into ¼-inch dice
¼ cup honeydew melon, peeled, seeded, and cut into ¼-inch dice
2 tablespoons cucumber, peeled, seeded, and cut into ⅛-inch dice
1½ tablespoons red bell pepper, seeded and cut into ¼-inch dice
1 large very ripe mango, peeled, seed removed, and coarsely chopped
1 fresh serrano chile, stemmed, seeded, and finely chopped
Juice of 1 lime
2 teaspoons finely chopped fresh cilantro
Salt and freshly ground black pepper to taste

1 In a medium-sized glass or ceramic bowl combine the jícama, melons, cucumber, and red pepper.

2 In a blender or food processor fitted with the metal blade, combine the mango, chile, and lime juice. Blend or process until smooth. Add to the chopped vegetables along with the cilantro, and season to taste with salt and pepper. Toss to mix. Cover and refrigerate until ready to serve.

Chipotle Lamb Chops with Creamed Corn Pudding and Three Tomato Salsas

SERVES 6
PREPARATION TIME: ABOUT 1 HOUR
COOKING TIME: ABOUT 1 HOUR
MARINATING TIME (SALSAS ONLY): ABOUT 30 MINUTES

These salsas do very well indeed made the morning before serving and refrigerated. Remember that they must be assembled at least 30 minutes before serving to give the flavors time to meld. If time or energy is a factor, make only one or two salsas, although the effect will not be quite as impressive.

3 tablespoons olive oil
½ cup chopped Vidalia or other sweet onion
¼ cup chopped carrot
2 tablespoons chopped celery
2 sprigs fresh thyme or ¾ teaspoon dried thyme
3 sprigs fresh rosemary
½ cup dry red wine
¾ cup veal or beef stock (see page 14)
2 teaspoons chipotle chile puree
2 tablespoons unsalted butter
Salt to taste
12 one-inch-thick rib lamp chops
Creamed Corn Pudding (recipe follows)
Tomatillo Salsa (recipe follows)
Red Tomato Salsa (recipe follows)
Yellow Tomato Salsa (recipe follows)

1 Prepare a medium-hot fire in charcoal or gas grill or pre-heat the broiler. If using a grill, toss a handful of soaked aromatic wood chips on the coals about 5 minutes before grilling the lamb chops. Assemble the *mise en place* trays for this recipes (see page 8).

2 Meanwhile, in a medium-sized saucepan, heat 2 tablespoons of the oil over medium heat. Add the onion, carrot, and celery and sauté for 4 to 5 minutes, until the vegetables soften a little. Add the thyme and 1 sprig of the rosemary and sauté for 1 minute more. Add the wine and cook for 10 minutes, or until the liquid is reduced to about 2 tablespoons. Lower the heat and add the stock and chile puree. Simmer for 3 minutes. Whisk in the butter, a tablespoon at a time, and season to taste with salt.

3 Strain the sauce through a fine sieve into the top half of a double boiler. Place over simmering water and keep warm until ready to serve.

4 Brush the lamb chops with the remaining 1 tablespoon of oil. Season to taste with salt. Toss the remaining 2 sprigs of rosemary on the charcoal. (If using a broiler, save the

STEPHAN PYLES: Chipotle Lamb Chops with Creamed Corn
Pudding and Three Tomato Salsas

rosemary for another use.) Grill the chops for about 6 to 8
minutes for medium rare, turning once.

5 Place a generous amount of Creamed Corn Pudding in
the center of warm serving plates. Place 2 lamb chops at
the edge of the pudding, crossing the bones over each
other. Drizzle the warm sauce over the chops. Garnish each
plate with a heaped tablespoon of each salsa. Pass extra
salsa on the side.

▶ Whether grilling or broiling, you may want to dip
rosemary sprigs in a little olive oil and brush lamb chops
several times during cooking.

CREAMED CORN PUDDING
SERVES 6

5 ears fresh corn, husks and silks removed
½ cup heavy cream
3 medium eggs
2 medium egg yolks
¼ cup diced red bell pepper
1 serrano chile, seeded and minced
1 tablespoon minced fresh cilantro
2 teaspoons pure maple syrup
⅛ teaspoon ground cinnamon
Salt and freshly ground black pepper to taste

1 Preheat the oven to 375 degrees F. Generously grease a
9-inch square baking dish with butter.

2 Using a sharp knife, cut the kernels from the corn into a
bowl. Scrape the cob to release all the milk. You should
have about 3 cups of corn.

3 In a another bowl, combine the cream, eggs, egg yolks,
bell pepper, chile, cilantro, maple syrup, and cinnamon
and beat well. Stir in the corn kernels and their milk and
season to taste with salt and pepper. Pour into the prepared
baking dish.

4 Bake for 25 to 35 minutes, or until a knife inserted into
the center comes out clean. Serve warm.

TOMATILLO SALSA
MAKES ABOUT 2 CUPS

8 tomatillos, husked, washed, and cut into ¼-inch dice
2 serrano chiles, seeded and finely diced
2 cloves garlic, roasted (see page 11), peeled and mashed
2 tablespoons finely chopped scallions
1 tablespoon finely chopped fresh cilantro
1 teaspoon fresh lime
Salt to taste

In a medium-sized glass or ceramic bowl, combine the
tomatillos and chiles. Stir in the garlic, scallions, cilantro,
and lime juice. Season to taste with salt. Let stand for at
least 30 minutes before serving.

RED TOMATO SALSA

MAKES ABOUT 1½ CUPS

4 small, ripe tomatoes, cored, seeded, and cut into ¼-inch dice
2 cloves garlic, roasted (see page 11), peeled and mashed
⅓ cup finely diced red onion
2 tablespoons finely diced red bell pepper
1 teaspoon fresh lime juice
Salt to taste

Put the tomatoes in a medium-sized glass or ceramic bowl. Stir in the garlic, onion, pepper, and lime juice. Season to taste with salt. Let stand for at least 30 minutes before serving.

YELLOW TOMATO SALSA

MAKES ABOUT 2 CUPS

4 small yellow tomatoes or 1½ to 2 cups yellow cherry tomatoes, cored, seeded, and cut into ¼-inch dice
2 serrano chiles, seeded and finely diced
3 tablespoons finely diced mango
2 tablespoons finely diced yellow bell pepper
2 to 3 teaspoons fresh orange juice
Salt to taste

In a medium-sized glass or ceramic bowl, combine the tomatoes, chiles, mango, bell pepper, and 2 teaspoons of orange juice. Season to taste with salt. Add more juice, if necessary. Let stand for at least 30 minutes before serving.

Cranberry-Mango Cobbler with Cinnamon-Pecan Cream

SERVES 6
PREPARATION TIME: ABOUT 30 MINUTES
BAKING TIME: ABOUT 1 HOUR
INFUSING AND COOKING TIME (CINNAMON-PECAN CREAM ONLY): ABOUT 50 MINUTES

If the end of summer is too early for the usual fall arrival of cranberries, check the freezer section of the supermarket, where cranberries are available all year long.

CRUMB TOPPING:

1 cup all-purpose flour
½ cup granulated sugar
½ cup packed light brown sugar
⅛ teaspoon freshly grated nutmeg
8 tablespoons (1 stick) cold, unsalted butter, cut into ½-inch pieces

COBBLER:

4 cups fresh or frozen cranberries, washed
1 cup plus ⅓ cup granulated sugar
2 cups all-purpose flour
2 teaspoons baking soda
½ teaspoon salt
1 cup (2 sticks) unsalted butter
1 large egg, lightly beaten
1 cup buttermilk
3 ripe mangoes, peeled, seeded, and diced (about 3½ cups)
Cinnamon-Pecan Cream (recipe follows)

■ Special Equipment: candy thermometer

1 Preheat the oven to 350 degrees F. Butter and flour a 9 x 12 x 2-inch baking dish. Assemble the *mise en place* trays for this recipe (see page 8).

2 To make the crumb topping, in a medium-sized bowl, combine the flour, granulated sugar, brown sugar, and nutmeg. With your fingers or a pastry blender, quickly blend in the butter until the mixture resembles coarse meal. Set aside.

3 To make the cobbler, in a bowl, combine the cranberries with 1 cup of the granulated sugar and set aside.

4 Sift together the flour, baking soda, and salt. Set aside.

5 In the bowl of an electric mixer, beat the butter and the remaining ⅓ cup sugar at high speed until light and fluffy. Beat in the beaten egg. Finally, stir in the flour mixture and the buttermilk, alternating the dry and liquid ingredients.

6 Spoon the batter into the prepared baking dish and smooth the top.

7 Gently toss the mangoes with the cranberries and spoon the fruit over the batter in an even layer. Sprinkle the reserved crumb topping over the fruit. Bake for 1 hour, or until the topping is crisp and light brown and the center is cooked through.

8 Remove the cobbler from the oven and allow to set for 10 minutes. Cut into squares and serve with the Cinnamon-Pecan Cream.

CINNAMON-PECAN CREAM
MAKES ABOUT 3 CUPS

2 cups milk
1 vanilla bean, split lengthwise
1 cup chopped toasted pecans
2 cinnamon sticks
6 large egg yolks
⅔ cup granulated sugar
⅔ cup heavy cream, whipped to soft peaks

1 In a large saucepan, combine the milk, vanilla bean, pecans, and cinnamon sticks. Bring to a boil over medium-high heat. Remove from the heat and set aside for 30 minutes to infuse.

2 In a large bowl, using an electric mixer set on high speed, beat the egg yolks and sugar until thick and pale.

3 Return the milk to the heat and bring to a boil. Strain through a fine sieve into the egg mixture, stirring constantly. Return the mixture to the pan and place over simmering water. Cook, stirring frequently, for about 20 minutes, or until the custard has thickened and a candy thermometer inserted into the center registers 180 degrees F.

4 Fill a very large bowl or pan with ice cubes. Set the pan of custard in the ice and stir in the whipped cream just until mixed. Allow to cool then pour into a bowl, cover and refrigerate until ready to serve.

STEPHAN PYLES: **Cranberry-Mango Cobbler with Cinnamon-Pecan Cream**

AN ELEGANT FALL DINNER, SOUTHWESTERN-STYLE

Chanterelles with Blue Corn Chips

Escalope of Salmon with Pepper-Ginger Medley

Grilled Beef Tenderloin with Tomatillo Sauce and
Blue Corn Crêpes

Passion Fruit Ice Cream with Raspberry Puree and
White Chocolate Sauce

WINE SUGGESTIONS:

Champagne or Sparkling Wine (*first course*)

Dry Riesling, Alsatian or German (*second course*)

Zinfandel or California Rhône-Style Wine (*third course*)

Jimmy Schmidt became a chef when he found himself enamored with the variety of colors and textures in the food combinations available throughout the United States. He is particularly fascinated by the flavors of foods served at the peak of their seasonality. This menu takes some time and effort to prepare, but many of the recipes can be done in stages—and the results will be well worth your work. This dinner really looks like fall, with the many hues of the ingredients reminiscent of the leaves changing into their autumnal glory.

◁ **Chanterelles with Blue Corn Chips**

WHAT YOU CAN PREPARE AHEAD OF TIME

One week ahead: Make the ginger sauce for the salmon. Cover and refrigerate. Make the Achiote Paste. Prepare the Blue Corn Crêpes and layer between pieces of wax paper. Wrap tightly in aluminum foil and freeze. To reheat, place on a baking sheet in a preheated 325 degree F. oven for 30 minutes. Make the Beef Stock. Make the Fish Stock.

Up to 2 days ahead: Make the Blue Corn Tortillas for the chips. Wrap in plastic wrap and refrigerate. Make the Passion Fruit Ice Cream. Make the Raspberry Puree. Cover and refrigerate.

Early in the day: Prepare the vegetables, herbs, and greens as instructed in the recipes. Make the White Chocolate Sauce.

In the afternoon: Chop the herbs. Prepare the cheese mixture for the Chanterelles with Blue Corn Chips. Cover and refrigerate. Bring to room temperature before using. Fry the Blue Corn Tortilla Chips.

Up to 2 hours before the party: If not already made, make the ginger sauce for the salmon. Keep warm. Marinate the salmon. Bring to room temperature before cooking.

Chanterelles with Blue Corn Chips

SERVES 6
PREPARATION TIME: ABOUT 10 MINUTES
COOKING TIME: ABOUT 7 MINUTES

These have got to be the world's most elegant nachos! With these as hors d'oeuvres and a glass of bubbly, you are on your way to a great party.

½ cup sour cream
¼ cup mild goat cheese, such as a Bucheron
Tabasco to taste
4 tablespoons unsalted butter
2 cups trimmed and cleaned chanterelles
24 fresh blue corn tortilla chips (see page 13) or store-bought, unsalted blue corn chips
¼ cup chopped fresh mint
¼ cup snipped fresh chives

1 Preheat the oven to 400 degrees F. Assemble the *mise en place* trays for this recipe (see page 8).

2 In a bowl, beat the sour cream and goat cheese until smooth. Season to taste with Tabasco. Set aside.

3 In a large skillet, melt the butter over high heat. Add the chanterelles and sauté for about 3 minutes, or until golden. Drain on paper towels and keep warm.

4 Spread the corn chips on an ungreased baking sheet. Generously spread the sour cream mixture on each chip. Bake on the lower rack of the oven for about 4 minutes, or until hot.

5 Sprinkle the chips with the mint and chives. Top with the chanterelles and serve immediately.

▶ **Always cook chanterelles quickly over high heat, or they will toughen. Substitute any cultivated "wild" mushrooms for the chanterelles if you cannot find them in the market.**

Escalope of Salmon with Pepper-Ginger Medley

SERVES 6
PREPARATION TIME: ABOUT 25 MINUTES
COOKING TIME: ABOUT 1 HOUR

The mildly spicy, marinated salmon resting on a bed of crisp greens, with its slightly acidic sauce, is a zinging rendition of the traditionally sedate fish course.

1½ cups chopped fresh ginger
½ cup fresh lemon juice
2 tablespoons granulated sugar
2 cups water
12 three-ounce salmon fillets, trimmed of dark flesh
⅓ cup Achiote Paste (see page 15)
2 tablespoons olive oil
½ cup finely julienned chayote squash (about ½ chayote)
1½ cups fish stock (see page 14)
1½ cups Chardonnay or other dry white wine
1½ cups heavy cream
1 red bell pepper, seeds and membranes removed, cut into fine julienne
1 yellow bell pepper, seeds and membranes removed, cut into fine julienne
Salt and freshly ground black pepper to taste
Juice of 1 lime
1 poblano chile, roasted (see page 10), peeled, seeded and diced
2 heads frisée (curly endive), trimmed, washed and dried
⅓ cup chopped fresh Italian parsley

1 Assemble the *mise en place* trays for this recipe (see page 8).

2 In a small saucepan, combine the ginger, lemon juice, sugar, and water. Bring to a boil over high heat. Reduce the heat and simmer, partially covered, for about 30 minutes, until slightly thickened. Transfer the mixture to a blender or food processor fitted with the metal blade. Blend or process until smooth. Strain through a fine sieve into a glass or ceramic bowl and discard the solids. Set aside.

▷ JIMMY SCHMIDT: Escalope of Salmon with Pepper-Ginger Medley

3 Rinse the salmon under cold, running water and pat dry on paper towels.

4 In a small bowl, combine 2 tablespoons of the ginger puree, the Achiote Paste, and the olive oil. Lay the salmon in a shallow container. Generously rub the ginger mixture over the salmon. Cover and refrigerate until ready to grill, but for no longer than 2 hours.

5 Blanch the chayote in a small saucepan of boiling water for 30 seconds. Refresh under cold, running water and set aside.

6 Prepare a charcoal or gas grill or preheat the broiler.

7 Meanwhile, in the top half of a double boiler, combine the stock and wine. Set over medium-high heat and bring to a simmer. Simmer for 20 to 25 minutes, or until reduced to ¼ cup. Add the cream and remaining ginger puree and simmer for 10 to 12 minutes more, or until the sauce is thick enough to coat the back of a spoon. Remove from the heat and set the top of the double boiler over very hot water. Cover to keep warm.

8 In a lightly oiled, nonstick skillet, sauté the red pepper over medium-high heat for 2 minutes. Add the yellow pepper and chayote and sauté for 1 minute more, or until hot.

Season to taste with salt and pepper. Remove from the heat and set aside.

9 Grill the salmon for 2 minutes. Turn it over and cook for 4 minutes more, or until medium rare. Do not overcook.

10 Meanwhile, test the sauce. If it is not hot, reheat the sauce in the double broiler over medium-high heat. Stir in the lime juice and diced poblano. Taste and adjust seasoning with salt and pepper, if necessary.

11 Arrange equal portions of the frisée and parsley leaves in the center of each plate. Sprinkle with the sautéed vegetables. Position salmon on top of peppers. Spoon the sauce over the salmon and serve immediately.

▶ The recipe is delicious made with skinless, boneless chicken breasts.

▶ If you don't have Achiote Paste on hand, you can substitute a mixture of 3 tablespoons mild Hungarian paprika, 3 tablespoons red bell pepper puree, and 1 tablespoon red wine vinegar.

Grilled Beef Tenderloin with Tomatillo Sauce and Blue Corn Crêpes

SERVES 6
PREPARATION TIME: ABOUT 25 MINUTES
COOKING TIME: ABOUT 1 HOUR AND 30 MINUTES
RESTING TIME (CRÊPE BATTER ONLY): 30 MINUTES

Jimmy Schmidt told us that this dish was inspired by his love of fajitas, which he felt were too much like peasant food to serve in a sophisticated Southwestern restaurant. Surely this interpretation of the traditional folk dish will shine at the most elegant dinner party.

8 to 10 tomatillos, husked, washed, and diced
1 cup heavy cream
1 tablespoon unsalted butter
2 cups diced red onions
2 cups red wine
2 cups Beef Stock (see page 14)
Salt to taste
12 three-ounce beef tenderloin steaks (filet mignon)
2 tablespoons ground cumin

½ cup diced, roasted red bell peppers (see page 10)
½ cup diced chipotle chiles in adobo sauce (see page 91)
2 tablespoons snipped chives
2 tablespoons chopped, fresh cilantro
12 Blue Corn Crêpes (recipe follows)
12 sprigs fresh cilantro

1 Assemble the *mise en place* trays for this recipe (see page 8).

2 In a small saucepan, combine ½ cup of the diced tomatillos and the cream. Bring to a simmer over medium heat and cook for about 10 minutes, or until the mixture is thick enough to coat the back of a spoon. Strain through a fine sieve into a small bowl, pressing on the solids. Discard the solids. Set aside.

JIMMY SCHMIDT: **Grilled Beef Tenderloin with Tomatillo Sauce and Blue Corn Crêpes**

3 In a saucepan, melt the butter over medium heat. Add the onions and sauté for about 5 minutes, or until translucent. Add the red wine and cook for about 20 minutes, or until the wine has completely evaporated. Transfer the mixture to a blender or food processor fitted with the metal blade. Blend or process until pureed. Strain through a fine sieve into a small bowl, pressing on the solids. Discard the solids. Set aside.

4 Prepare a charcoal or gas grill or preheat the broiler.

5 Meanwhile, in a large saucepan, bring the stock to a simmer over high heat. Reduce the heat and simmer for about 10 minutes, or until reduced to 1 cup. Add the tomatillo cream and red onion puree. Season to taste with salt. Pour into the top half of a double boiler set over hot water, cover and and keep warm.

6 Rub the beef steaks with the cumin. Grill the beef, turning once, for 4 to 5 minutes for rare. Cook for an additional 2 minutes for medium and an additional 4 to 6 minutes for well done.

7 Stir the remaining diced tomatillos, the roasted peppers, chipotles, chives, and chopped cilantro into the sauce. Place a warm crêpe in the center of each warm dinner plate. Place 2 fillets, overlapping slightly, on the lower half of each crêpe. Spoon a little sauce over the top, then fold the crêpe over the meat. Garnish with the sprigs of cilantro and serve immediately.

BLUE CORN CRÊPES
MAKES 16 CRÊPES

½ cup all-purpose flour
6 large eggs, beaten
1 cup stone-ground blue cornmeal
⅔ cup milk
1 teaspoon salt
Unsalted butter, for cooking the crêpes

■ Special Equipment: nonstick 6-inch crêpe pan

1 In a medium-sized bowl, beat the flour and eggs together.

2 In another bowl, beat the cornmeal and milk together. When well combined, whisk into the flour and egg mixture, and stir in the salt. Cover and let the batter rest for 30 minutes.

3 In a 6-inch, nonstick crêpe pan or skillet, melt about ¼ teaspoon of butter over medium-high heat. Using a 1-ounce ladle (⅛ cup measuring cup), add just enough crêpe batter to cover the bottom of the pan, tilting it to allow the batter to spread evenly. Cook for about 1 minute, or until lightly browned. Flip the crêpe and cook the other side for 1 minute.

4 Transfer the crêpe to a piece of wax paper. Continue to make the crêpes, adding half-teaspoons of butter to the pan as needed. Layer the cooked crêpes between wax paper and keep warm.

Passion Fruit Ice Cream with Raspberry Puree and White Chocolate Sauce

This dessert is a true indulgence with the tropical perfume of the passion fruit enhanced by the rich white chocolate sauce and delicate raspberry puree—certainly an exotic end to a most cosmopolitan meal.

ICE CREAM:

2½ cups passion fruit puree
½ cup granulated sugar
8 large egg yolks
1 teaspoon pure vanilla extract
⅛ teaspoon salt
2 cups heavy cream

RASPBERRY PUREE:

1 pint fresh raspberries

SAUCE:

1 cup half-and-half
1 tablespoon chopped cassia buds (or 2 three-inch cinnamon sticks, broken into pieces)
3 large egg yolks
2 tablespoons granulated sugar
1 teaspoon pure vanilla extract
⅛ teaspoon salt
5 ounces white chocolate, finely chopped
½ cup heavy cream
6 sprigs fresh mint

■ Special Equipment: ice cream maker

1 Assemble the *mise en place* trays for this recipe (see page 8).

2 To make the ice cream, in a medium-sized saucepan, combine the passion fruit puree, sugar, egg yolks, vanilla extract, and salt. Cook over medium-low heat, stirring continuously, for 10 minutes, or until the mixture is thick enough to coat the back of a spoon. Do not allow to boil.

3 Remove from the heat and add the cream. Strain through a fine sieve into a bowl. Cool until tepid, cover and refrigerate for at least 2 hours until cold.

4 Pour the passion fruit mixture into an ice cream maker and process according to the manufacturer's directions. When frozen, scrape into a freezer container with a lid,

cover, and freeze for at least 8 hours for a firm texture.

5 To make the raspberry puree, put the berries in a blender or food processor fitted with the metal blade. Puree and strain through a fine sieve into a small bowl. Cover and refrigerate.

6 To make the white chocolate sauce, heat the half-and-half in a small saucepan over medium heat until bubbles form around the edges. Do not boil. Remove from the heat and add the cassia. Allow to cool.

7 In a bowl, whisk together the egg yolks, sugar, vanilla, and salt.

8 Strain the half-and-half, return it to the saucepan and heat again until bubbles form around the edges. Remove from the heat and whisk a few tablespoons into the egg mixture. Add the rest of the hot half-and-half to the egg mixture, whisking continuously. Transfer the mixture to the saucepan and cook over medium heat for about 5 minutes, or until thick enough to coat the back of a spoon. Do not boil.

9 Remove the pan from the heat, add the chopped chocolate, and stir continuously until melted. Stir in the cream, and strain through a fine sieve into a bowl. Cool until tepid, cover and refrigerate until ready to use.

10 To serve, spoon a little of the sauce into the center of each of 6 small dessert plates or shallow bowls. Drizzle with the raspberry puree. Place a scoop of ice cream in the center of the sauce. Garnish with the mint sprigs and serve immediately.

▶ **Passion fruit puree is available in the frozen food section of specialty food stores. It is also sold through restaurant supply companies. According to Chef Schmidt, one fresh passion fruit will yield only about 2 tablespoons of puree, so the frozen is the most economical.**

▶ **Leftover white chocolate sauce will keep in a tightly sealed jar in the refrigerator for up to 2 days. Leftover ice cream will keep in the freezer for up to 2 weeks.**

▷ JIMMY SCHMIDT: Passion Fruit Ice Cream with Raspberry Puree and White Chocolate Sauce

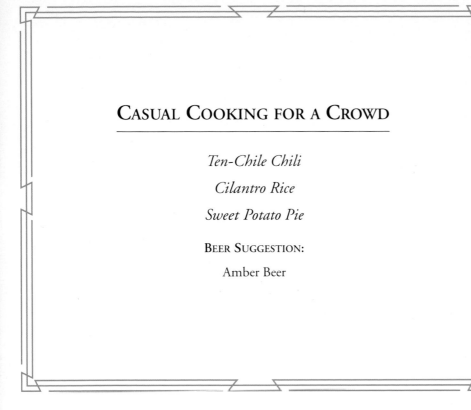

CASUAL COOKING FOR A CROWD

Ten-Chile Chili

Cilantro Rice

Sweet Potato Pie

BEER SUGGESTION:

Amber Beer

WHAT YOU CAN PREPARE AHEAD OF TIME

Up to 1 week ahead: Make the Beef or Chicken Stock. Make the Chili. Cool, transfer to a freezer container, cover well and freeze. Partially thaw at room temperature, and then gently reheat in a large Dutch oven. Prepare the pie shell and freeze.

Up to 3 days ahead: If not already made, make the Chili. Cool, cover, and refrigerate.

Early in the day: Dice the peppers for the Cilantro Rice. Cover and refrigerate. Prepare the puree for the Sweet Potato Pie. Bake the pie shell.

In the afternoon: Cook the Cilantro Rice. Cover and let stand at room temperature. Bake the Sweet Potato Pie.

Brendan Walsh was the pioneer of Southwestern cooking in New York City at the legendary Arizona 206. Brendan grew up in the Bronx, a far cry from the deserts of Arizona and New Mexico, but when his love of cooking led him to study French cooking with an emphasis on the foods of the South of France, it seemed a logical step to investigate the lively cuisine of America's Southwest. As with everything he does, Brendan plunged into this style of cooking with exuberant enthusiasm. He has had such a good time learning that he especially enjoys teaching—give him a crowd of food enthusiasts and he will share all his culinary secrets!

This menu brings a taste of the Southwest to a football weekend crowd or any large group you have gathered for informal entertaining. The chili is, without question, the Super Bowl of chilies, especially when teamed with cilantro-flavored rice and a down-home Sweet Potato Pie. All you need to add is a big green salad and plenty of Mexican beer to score a cook's touchdown.

◁ Ten-Chile Chili and Cilantro Rice

Ten-Chile Chili

Brendan's chili calls for 10 chiles, with each one impart-ing its own special aromatic scent to the final dish. The chef says that this is one instance when more is better! I agree. However, if you cannot find all of the chiles, don't panic. Simply up the quantity of those you can find. The dish will still taste very good. This recipe serves at least 12 hungry people, so it is the perect chili to make when you are expecting a crowd.

3 pounds Spanish onions, chopped
¾ pound slab bacon, diced
5 pounds lean beef chuck, trimmed and cut into ¼-inch by 1½-inch strips
¾ cup diced celery
½ cup chopped dried mulato chiles
½ cup chopped dried pasilla chiles
½ cup chopped dried ancho chiles
5 dried chiles pequín
1 cup ancho chile powder (see page 10)
⅓ cup ground toasted coriander seeds (see page 10)
⅓ cup ground cumin seeds (see page 11)
1 tablespoon plus 2 teaspoons cayenne pepper
5 bay leaves
4 cups peeled, seeded, and chopped ripe plum tomatoes
2 cups Beef or Chicken Stock (see pages 13 and 14)
½ cup tequila, such as Cuervo Gold
¼ cup seeded, minced serrano chiles
¼ cup seeded, minced jalapeño chiles
3½ ounces canned chipotle chiles in adobo (see page 91), chopped (half of a seven-ounce can)
1 smoked ham hock
1 sprig fresh rosemary
1 sprig fresh sage
1 sprig fresh oregano
Salt to taste

GARNISH:

1 tablespoon olive oil
1 cup seeded, julienned red bell peppers
1 cup seeded, julienned yellow bell peppers
1 cup seeded, julienned poblano chiles
1 cup seeded, julienned Anaheim chiles
1 jalapeño chile, seeded and julienned

■ Special Equipment: large Dutch oven

1 Assemble the *mise en place* trays for this recipe (see page 8).

2 In a large Dutch oven, cook the bacon, stirring frequent-ly, over medium-high heat for 5 minutes, or until the fat is rendered. Using a slotted spoon, remove the bacon and drain on paper towels. Drain off all but 2 to 3 tablespoons of bacon fat.

3 Add a quarter of the beef to the pot and cook, stirring, for 2 to 3 minutes. Remove the meat and drain on paper towels. Repeat with the remaining meat, cooking in batches.

4 When all the meat has been browned, add the onions to the pot. Lower the heat and cook, stirring frequently, for 15 to 20 minutes, or until caramelized. Add the celery and cook for 4 to 5 minutes, or until tender.

5 Return the meat to the pot. Stir in the chopped dried chiles, chiles pequín, chile powder, ground coriander, ground cumin, cayenne, and bay leaves. Add the tomatoes, stock, and tequila and stir to blend. Stir in the minced chiles, chipotle chiles, ham hock, rosemary, sage, and oregano. Raise the heat and bring to a simmer. Reduce the heat to medium-low and cook, partially covered, for 6 hours, stirring occasionally, or until the chili is thick and the flavors are intensely blended. Taste and add salt, if necessary.

6 To prepare the garnish, about 20 minutes before the chili is ready, heat the olive oil in a large saucepan over medium-high heat. Add the julienned bell peppers and chiles and sauté for 4 to 5 minutes, or until just softened. Remove from the heat, cover to keep warm, and set aside.

7 To serve, remove the ham hock, bay leaves, and herb sprigs from the chili. Serve the chili in bowls, topped with a spoonful of julienned peppers. Serve the Cilantro Rice on the side.

▶ **Fresh tomatoes can be replaced with chopped, canned Italian plum tomatoes. The ham hock can be replaced with 1 smoked turkey leg.**

Cilantro Rice

Brendan's method for cooking rice should yield perfectly cooked rice every time. His addition of pungent cilantro adds a whole new dimension to plain boiled white rice while giving it a flavor readily associated with Southwestern cooking. This rice can be served warm or at room temperature as a well-seasoned salad.

8 cups cold water
4 cups long-grain white rice
1 tablespoon plus 1 teaspoon coarse salt
3 cups chopped fresh cilantro
2 cups diced red bell peppers
2 cups diced yellow bell peppers
1 cup olive oil
⅔ cup white wine vinegar
Freshly ground black pepper to taste

1 Assemble the *mise en place* trays for this recipe (see page 8).

2 In a large saucepan, bring the water to a boil over high heat. Add the rice and salt and bring back to a boil. Immediately lower the heat, cover the pan, and cook for 20 minutes. Remove from the heat and let rest, covered, for 10 minutes.

3 Transfer the rice to a large bowl. Stir in the cilantro, bell peppers, olive oil, vinegar, and pepper to taste. Serve immediately or cover and let stand at room temperature.

▶ **This recipe can be easily tripled for a large crowd.**

▶ **Fresh basil or parsley may be substituted for cilantro.**

BRENDAN WALSH: Cilantro Rice

Sweet Potato Pie

Borrowing from the cooking of America's South, Chef Walsh prepares Sweet Potato Pie as the perfect ending to a winning meal. Cut this rich pie into thin wedges and serve with a generous scoop of vanilla ice cream alongside, or, if you want more dessert, bake two pies.

PIE PASTRY:

1½ cups all-purpose flour
¼ teaspoon salt
½ cup solid vegetable shortening, chilled
3 to 4 tablespoons ice water

FILLING:

2 pounds sweet potatoes, peeled and cubed
¼ teaspoon salt
2 tablespoons unsalted butter
½ cup honey
¼ cup packed light brown sugar
1 tablespoon dark rum
1 teaspoon ground cinnamon
⅛ teaspoon freshly grated nutmeg
3 large eggs, lightly beaten
½ cup heavy cream, whipped to soft peaks

■ Special equipment: 9-inch pie plate; pie weights

1 Assemble the *mise en place* trays for this recipe (see page 8).

2 To make the pastry, in a medium-sized bowl, combine the flour and salt. With your fingertips or a pastry blender, blend in the shortening until the mixture resembles coarse meal. Add the water, a tablespoon at a time, blending lightly after each addition, until the dough just holds together. Roll the pastry into a ball and flatten slightly. Wrap in plastic wrap and refrigerate for at least 2 hours.

3 Meanwhile, to make the filling, put the sweet potatoes and salt in a saucepan and add enough cold water to cover by several inches. Bring to a boil, lower the heat, and simmer for about 15 minutes, until the potatoes are very tender when pierced with a fork. Drain well.

4 Transfer the drained potatoes to a blender or a food processor fitted with the metal blade. Blend or process until smooth. Transfer the puree to a bowl and allow to cool for 5 minutes.

5 Stir the butter, honey, brown sugar, rum, and spices into the sweet potato puree until well blended. Cover and set aside.

6 Preheat the oven to 425 degrees F.

7 To continue making the pie pastry, roll out the pastry on a lightly floured surface or between 2 sheets of plastic wrap to circle about 12 inches in diameter and ⅛-inch thick. Line a 9-inch pie plate with the pastry so that it overhangs the edges by about 1 inch. Trim the edges and crimp lightly. Prick the bottom of the pastry with a fork.

8 Line the pastry with cooking parchment or aluminum foil and fill with pie weights, dried beans, or rice. Bake for 5 minutes. Remove the weights and parchment and bake for 4 minutes more. The pastry will barely begin to brown. Remove from the oven and cool on a wire rack. Lower the oven temperature to 350 degrees F.

9 Finish making the filling by putting the eggs in the top half of a double boiler over gently simmering water. Using a hand-held electric mixer set on high speed, or a whisk, beat the eggs for 5 minutes, or until very pale and thick. Do not let the water boil or the eggs may scramble.

10 Fold the eggs into the sweet potato puree until well incorporated. Gently fold in the whipped cream.

11 Pour the filling into the partially baked pie shell. Bake for approximately 1 hour and 15 minutes, or until the filling is golden brown on top and set. Transfer to a wire rack and cool before serving.

▷ BRENDAN WALSH: Sweet Potato Pie

A SOUTHWESTERN THANKSGIVING

*Guajillo-Maple Glazed Turkey
with Sautéed Greens, Beets and Yams*

Apricot-Peach Chutney

Black Pepper-Scallion Cornbread

Lemon Anise Churros

WINE SUGGESTIONS:

Sparkling Wine

Cru Beaujolais

Zinfandel

(may be served throughout)

WHAT YOU CAN PREPARE AHEAD OF TIME

Up to 1 week ahead: Make the Apricot-Peach Chutney. Cover and refrigerate.

Up to 2 days ahead: Make the Guajillo-Maple Glaze. Cover and refrigerate. Reheat before using.

The day before: Wash and trim the beet greens. Wrap in wet paper towels, place in a sealed plastic bag, and refrigerate. Cook and cool beets and yams. Cover and refrigerate.

Early in the day: Make the Black Pepper-Scallion Cornbread. Reheat in a preheated 200 degrees F. oven for 10 minutes before serving.

David Walzog is the latest in our list of most impressive chefs from Arizona 206 in New York City. His intense infatuation with Southwestern cooking is infectious. This is deliciously illustrated in his Thanksgiving menu, which emphasizes the use of traditional ingredients in a very contemporary way. Turkey and all the trimmings—beets, yams, and cornbread—are here but the meal is designed to incorporate the best of the lively ingredients we associate with the sun-drenched flavors of western Texas, New Mexico, and Arizona. The meal does not turn its back on New England and the familiar fare, it simply rejoices in the great diversity of our expansive and always inventive country.

◁ (From left to right) Black Pepper-Scallion Cornbread; Lemon Anise Churros; Guajillo-Maple Glazed Turkey with Sautéed Greens, Beets, and Yams; and Apricot-Peach Chutney

Guajillo-Maple Glazed Turkey with Sautéed Greens, Beets, and Yams

SERVES 6
PREPARATION TIME: ABOUT 45 MINUTES
COOKING TIME: ABOUT 5 HOURS AND 30 MINUTES

The sweet-and-spicy glaze keeps the turkey moist and adds enormous zest to the mild-flavored bird. The beautiful color of the glazed skin is further accentuated by the rich red and gold of the vegetables.

GLAZE:

2 large turkey legs
3 heads garlic, halved crosswise
2½ cups pure maple syrup
1 cup chopped white onions
5 sprigs fresh thyme
5 sprigs fresh rosemary
4 cups chicken stock (see page 13)
½ cup guajillo chile puree (see page 10)
1 cup water

TURKEY:

1 fourteen-pound fresh turkey
4 heads garlic, halved crosswise
About 10 sprigs fresh thyme
About 10 sprigs fresh rosemary
Salt and freshly ground black pepper to taste

VEGETABLES:

5 large yams, washed
6 large beets, washed
3 bunches beet greens, trimmed, washed, and dried
4 tablespoons unsalted butter

■ **Special Equipment: small melon-baller**

1 Preheat the oven to 425 degrees F. Assemble the *mise en place* trays for this recipe (see page 8).

2 To make the glaze, split the turkey legs open with a sharp knife and pull apart to butterfly them. Place in a roasting pan and cook for about 1 hour, or until very brown, draining off the fat periodically.

3 Add the garlic, maple syrup, onion, and thyme and rosemary sprigs, and continue to roast for 20 minutes. Reduce the oven temperature to 325 F.

4 Transfer the contents of the roasting pan to a large, heavy saucepan. Stir in the stock, chile puree, and water. Bring to a boil over medium-high heat. Reduce the heat and simmer for 30 minutes.

5 Strain the glaze through a fine sieve into a smaller saucepan. Set aside and keep warm.

6 To roast the turkey, rinse it and pat it dry with paper towels. Put the halved garlic heads, thyme, and rosemary into the cavity. Sprinkle, inside and out, with salt and pepper. Press the legs against the breast and tie in place using kitchen twine. Tuck the wings under the back. Set the turkey on a rack in the roasting pan. Cover the turkey with aluminum foil and roast for 1 hour and 30 minutes.

7 Remove the foil and continue to roast the turkey, basting every 15 minutes with the glaze, for about 2 hours longer, or until the juices run clear when the thigh is pierced with a fork. Remove from the oven and let rest for about 15 minutes before carving.

8 Meanwhile, prepare the vegetables: In separate saucepans, cook the yams and beets in boiling, salted water to cover by several inches for about 20 minutes, or until tender when pierced with a fork. Drain well and allow to cool.

9 Carefully peel the vegetables. Using a small melon-baller, scoop out balls from each vegetable, using as much of the flesh as you can. Set the balls aside in separate bowls.

10 Just before serving, in a large saucepan, melt 2 tablespoons of the butter over medium heat. Add the beet greens, cover and cook for about 2 minutes, or until wilted. Remove from the pan and keep warm.

11 Add the remaining 2 tablespoons of butter and 1 tablespoon of water to the saucepan. When the butter melts, add the reserved vegetable balls. Cook for 1 minute, or until the vegetables are heated through.

12 Place the turkey on a warm serving platter and surround with the vegetables. Reheat and pass the remaining glaze on the side.

▶ **If you don't have a melon-baller, cut the beets and yams into 1-inch cubes.**

▷ DAVID WALZOG: Guajillo-Maple Glazed Turkey with Sautéed Greens, Beets, and Yams

Apricot-Peach Chutney

What a treat! Homemade chutney replacing the usual cranberry sauce as a relish for the holiday bird. This is typical of David's fresh approach to Thanksgiving dinner. The hint of spice further complements the chile-glazed turkey.

9 ounces dried apricot halves, sliced (about 1½ cups)
4½ ounces dried black currants (about 1 cup)
2 ounces dried cranberries (about ½ cup)
1½ cups apricot puree (organic apricot puree, sold as baby food in natural food stores)
1 cup rice wine vinegar
¾ cup Triple Sec
2 cups water
1 serrano chile, stemmed, seeded, and chopped
2 tablespoons ancho chile powder (see page 10)
1 tablespoon salt
1½ teaspoons freshly ground black pepper
1 cup diced fresh peaches
⅔ cup chopped, toasted pecans
2 teaspoons chopped fresh thyme

1 Assemble the *mise en place* trays for this recipe (see page 8).

2 In a large, nonreactive saucepan, combine the apricots, black currants, cranberries, apricot puree, vinegar, Triple Sec, and water. Bring to a boil over high heat. Stir in the chile, chile powder, salt, and pepper. Reduce the heat to medium-low, cover and cook for 30 minutes, or until the dried fruits are very soft.

3 Strain the fruit through a fine sieve, reserving the liquid. Put the fruit in a medium-sized glass or ceramic bowl.

4 Return the liquid to the pan and cook over medium-high heat, stirring occasionally, for 5 minutes, or until a very thick syrup forms. (You should have about about 1½ cups.)

5 Pour the syrup over the fruit. Stir in the peaches, pecans, and thyme. Cover and refrigerate for at least 3 hours. Bring to room temperature before serving.

▶ To toast the pecans, lay them in a single layer on a baking sheet and toast in a preheated 400 degree F. oven. Toast for 5 to 10 minutes, or until golden. Immediately transfer to a plate to cool.

▶ To make apricot puree, cook ½ pound (1½ cups) of dried apricots in 2 cups of gently simmering water until soft. Transfer the apricots and liquid to a blender or food processor fitted with the metal blade. Blend or process until pureed.

▶ Substitute unsweetened frozen peaches for fresh. Thaw before adding to the chutney.

Black Pepper-Scallion Cornbread

5 tablespoons unsalted butter

1⅓ cups yellow stone-ground cornmeal

¾ cup all-purpose flour

2½ tablespoons granulated sugar

1 tablespoon salt

1 tablespoon plus 1 teaspoon baking powder

½ teaspoon baking soda

1 cup milk

1 large egg

½ cup chopped scallions (white parts only)

1 tablespoon cracked black pepper

■ Special Equipment: 9-inch round cake pan

1 Preheat the oven to 425 degrees F. Assemble the *mise en place* trays for this recipe (see page 8).

2 In a small saucepan, melt 4 tablespoons of the butter. Remove from the heat.

3 Put the remaining 1 tablespoon of butter in a 9-inch round cake pan and heat in the oven while preparing the cornbread batter.

4 In a medium-sized bowl, sift together the cornmeal, flour, sugar, salt, baking powder, and baking soda.

5 In another bowl, whisk the milk, egg, and melted butter together. Add to the cornmeal mixture and stir just to combine. Stir in the scallions and pepper.

6 Take the hot cake pan from the oven and tilt it to distribute the melted butter. Immediately pour the batter into the pan.

7 Bake for about 25 minutes, or until a cake tester inserted into the center comes out clean.

▶ Heating the butter and the pan helps brown the bread. The batter will sizzle when poured into the hot pan. If possible, use a dark-colored cake pan.

DAVID WALZOG: Black Pepper-Scallion Cornbread

Lemon Anise Churros

These are David's version of traditional folk fare snacks, with the lemon and anise adding a refreshing lightness. Since these have to be made at the last minute, allow some time between the end of the meal and dessert.

1¼ cups all-purpose flour
⅛ teaspoon salt
1 cup water
8 tablespoons (1 stick) unsalted butter
2 teaspoons ground star anise
Grated zest of 1 lemon
4 large eggs
1 cup granulated sugar
1 cup confectioners' sugar
Vegetable oil, for deep-frying

■ Special Equipment: deep-fat fryer, deep-fry thermometer, pastry bag with a medium star tip

1 Assemble the *mise en place* trays for this recipe (see page 8).

2 Sift together the flour and salt into a medium-sized bowl.

3 In a medium-sized saucepan, combine the water, butter, anise, and lemon zest. Bring to a boil over high heat. Immediately stir in the flour mixture and cook, beating constantly with a wooden spoon, until the mixture forms a ball and pulls away from the sides of the pan. Remove the pan from the heat.

4 Beat in the eggs, one at a time until they are well incorporated and the batter is smooth.

5 Combine the sugars in a plastic bag and set aside.

6 Spoon the batter into a pastry bag fitted with a medium-sized star tip.

7 Heat the oil in a deep-fat fryer to 375 degrees F. on a deep-fry thermometer. Or pour enough oil into a large heavy pan to reach a depth of 3 inches and heat to 375 degrees F.

8 Pipe the batter into the hot oil in 5- to 6-inch lengths, being careful not to crowd the pan. Fry for about 3 min-

utes, or until golden brown, turning once with tongs. Remove from the oil with a long-handled slotted spoon or tongs and drain well on paper towels. Continue frying until all the batter is used. Make sure the oil reaches the correct frying temperature between batches.

9 While they are still warm, drop the churros into the bag of sugar. Shake the bag to coat the churros generously with sugar. Serve warm.

▶ **These are also great breakfast treats served with a steaming cup of Mexican coffee.**

DAVID WALZOG: Lemon Anise Churros

Glossary

Achiote seeds: Rusty red seeds of the annatto tree. Used ground or whole to impart a rather musky flavor and a red-to-yellow color to foods. Often called annatto in Hispanic markets.

Anaheim: Long green chile ranging from mild to barely hot and also called *chile verde*. When dried, also known as *chile Colorado*.

Ancho: Long, dark brown, mildly hot, sweet dried chile, also called *chile negro*. When fresh, it's color ranges from dark green to dark red and it is known as poblano. Best toasted before using. Ancho chile powder is available in Hispanic and other markets.

Anisette: A sweet, clear, licorice-flavored liqueur made from anise seeds.

Annatto: See Achiote.

Árbol: Long, thin, bright orange, very hot chile. Used fresh or dried, it is known by the same name.

Banana: Mild yellow chile always used fresh. When mature, it turns bright red.

Blue corn masa: See Masa.

Cassia buds: The bud of cassia is slightly more pungent and bitter than the more familiar Ceylon cinnamon, which can replace it. Cassia buds are sold in specialty and Hispanic markets.

Chayote: A mild, thin-skinned, pale green squash that can be eaten raw or cooked. It is pear-shaped with a white interior, and is also known as christophene or mirliton.

Chile in adobo: Canned chiles, usually chipotle chiles, preserved in a tomato-based sauce (see Chipotle).

Chile powder: A deep red ground seasoning mix combining chiles, herbs, spices, garlic, and salt that may be mild, hot, or in between.

Chiles: Mild to very hot vegetables ranging in color from pale yellow and green to bright red. There are estimated to be more than 500 varieties of chiles grown worldwide. Try to find the type called for in a particular recipe, but if that is impossible, substitute a similar chile—one that is about the same size and has the same degree of heat.

Chipotle: Dried smoked jalapeño chile. It is extremely hot and often is prepared in adobo sauce, a mixture of tomatoes, onions, vinegar, and spices. Canned chipotle chiles in adobo sauce are sold in Hispanic and specialty markets.

Chorizo: Flavorful pork sausage seasoned with garlic, onion, chile powder, spices, and vinegar. Used extensively in Hispanic cooking.

Churro: Slightly sweet, doughnut-like Spanish pastry. Usually served as a snack with coffee.

Cilantro: Pungent herb that looks like flat-leaf parsley, used to flavor Asian, Indian, and Latin American dishes. The bright green leaves are sometimes referred to as Chinese parsley or fresh coriander. Cilantro is widely available. There is no substitute. Do not use coriander seeds instead!

Corn husks: Dried husks from large ears of corn that are soaked and used as wrappings for tamales. They are not meant to be eaten. Available in Hispanic and specialty markets.

Cremini mushrooms: Cocoa-colored, firm textured, intensely flavorful cultivated "wild" mushrooms.

Enchilada: A tortilla that is often dipped in a chile-seasoned sauce and then rolled up or folded over a filling.

Epazote: A wild herb with flat, pointed leaves and a strong, well-defined, pungent taste, used primarily in Mexican cooking. It is often used to flavor beans, as it is said to reduce gas. Also known as wormweed.

Fresno: Fairly mild, triangular-shaped chile that usually is marketed green, although it can be yellow or red when mature.

Guajillo: Long, thin, dark red, extremely hot and flavorful dried chile. When fresh, it is called mirasol.

Habanero: Small, ridged, round, exceedingly hot chile that is related to the scotch bonnet and usually sold when green and immature, but also may be available yellow, orange, or red. This is the hottest chile.

Jalapeño: Small, triangular-shaped, hot green chile. Can be bright red when mature. Jalapeños are often sold pickled.

Jícama: A large brown-skinned root vegetable with a sweet, crisp white interior, eaten both raw and cooked. Readily available in Hispanic markets and many mainstream supermarkets.

Mango: A thick-skinned tropical fruit with a huge seed and succulent, sweet, soft, orange pulp. Mangos may be round, oblong, or kidney-shaped, and range in weight from six ounces to five pounds.

Masa: Cornmeal dough traditionally used to make tortillas. Masa may be blue or yellow.

Masa harina: Flour made from dried masa.

Mexican oregano: An herb from the verbena family with a long, fuzzy, deeply veined leaf. It should not be replaced by the familiar Mediterranean oregano. Look for it in greengrocers, Hispanic markets, and specialty shops.

Mirasol: See Guajillo.

Mulato: Long, very dark brown, mildly hot and sweet dried chile. Similar to ancho in use.

New Mexico: Fairly large, red or green, mildly hot chile, used fresh or dried.

Papaya: A tropical to semitropical pear-shaped fruit with greenish-yellow skin and a golden-orange or red-orange interior. Both the juicy, tart-sweet flesh and the spicy black seeds are edible.

Pasilla: Long, thin, hot dried chile.

Pequín: A tiny, fiery, red chile, that can be used fresh or dried.

Poblano: Long, mildly hot, dark green chile. When dried, it is known as ancho.

Portobello mushrooms: Cremini (see Cremini) mushrooms that are allowed to mature to large open-gill mushrooms with a deep umber, dense, somewhat fibrous flesh.

Quesadilla: A filled tortilla, folded into a turnover shape and either toasted or fried. Often served as an appetizer.

Sambuca: An anise-flavored Italian liqueur, usually served straight up with a few coffee beans floating on the top.

Scotch bonnet: Related to the habanero but smaller. Sold fresh in bright colors ranging from green to yellow, orange and red. Very hot.

Serrano: Small, red or green, very hot chile. Always used fresh.

Shiitake mushroom: Cultivated, full-flavored, dark brown "wild" mushrooms with broad caps ranging from 3- to 10-inches in diameter. Widely available both fresh and dried.

Star anise: A dried, star-shaped pod filled with tiny, pungent seeds. The licorice-flavored spice is used mainly in Asian cooking and is most easily found in Asian markets.

Taco: A tortilla, usually fried, folded over a meat, poultry, or bean filling and garnished with salad-type trimmings.

Tamale: A savory filling encased in dough, wrapped in corn husks, and steamed.

Tomatillo: A light green, plum-sized, astringent fruit covered with a fine, paper-like husk, related to the cape gooseberry. Tomatillos are primarily used either roasted or boiled in Mexican green sauces. Although they are sometimes called Mexican tomatoes, green tomatoes cannot be substituted for them. Tomatillos are widely available in Hispanic markets and many mainstream supermarkets.

Tostada: A crisply fried tortilla; also, a fried tortilla covered with a savory topping.

Sources for Dried Chiles & Spices, etc.

The CMC Company, P.O. Drawer B, Avalon, NJ 08202. (800) 262-2780. Catalog available, checks only.

Don Alfonso Foods, P.O. Box 201988, Austin, TX 78720-1988. (800) 456-6100. Catalog available.

Los Chileros de Nuevo Mexico, P.O. Box 6215, Santa Fe, NM 87502. (505) 471-6968. Catalog available, checks only.

Mo Hotta-Mo Betta, P.O. Box 4136, San Luis Obispo, CA 93403. (800) 462-3200. Catalog available.

Old Southwest Trading Company, P.O. Box 7545, Albuquerque, NM 87194. (505) 836-0168. Catalog available.

Hot Stuff Spicy Food Store, 227 Sullivan Street, New York, NY 10012. (800) 466-8206 / (212) 254-6120.

The Kitchen, 218 Eighth Avenue, New York, NY 10011. (212) 243-4433.

Dean & Deluca, 560 Broadway, New York, NY 10012. (800) 221-7714 / (212) 431-1691.

Balducci's, 424 Avenue of the Americas, New York, NY 10011. (212) 673-2600.

Balducci's Mail Order Division, 1102 Queens Plaza South, Long Island City, NY 11101. (800) BALDUCCI.

The Chile Shop, 109 East Water Street, Sante Fe, NM 87501. (505) 983-6080.

Texas Spice Company, P.O. Box 3769, Austin, TX 78764-3769. (800) 880-8007 / (512) 444-2223.

Carmen's of New Mexico, 401 Mountain Road NW, Albuquerque, NM 07102. (800) 851-4852.

Penzey's Spice House Ltd., P.O. Box 1448, Waukesha, WI 53187. (414) 574-0277. Catalog available.

Harry Wils & Co., Inc. (For Passion Fruit Puree), 182 Duane Street, New York, NY 10013. (212) 431-9731. Catalog available.

Index

Conversion Chart

Weights and Measures

1 teaspoon = 5 milliliters

1 tablespoon = 3 teaspoons = 15 milliliters

1/8 cup = 2 tablespoons = 1 fluid ounce = 30 milliliters

1/4 cup = 4 tablespons = 2 fluid ounces = 60 milliliters

1/2 cup = 8 tablespoons = 4 fluid ounces = 120 milliliters

1 cup = 16 tablespoons = 8 fluid ounces = 240 milliliters

1 pint = 2 cups = 16 fluid ounces = 480 milliliters

1 quart = 4 cups = 32 fluid ounces = 960 milliliters (.96 liter)

1 gallon = 4 quarts = 16 cups = 128 fluid ounces = 3.84 liters

1 ounce = 28 grams

1/4 pound = 4 ounces = 114 grams

1 pound = 16 ounces = 454 grams

2.2 pounds = 1,000 grams = 1 kilogram